Praise for *Microinteractions*

"*Microinteractions* is a book I've wanted for a very long time. I've needed a thoughtful, insightful, and concise understanding of how to look at interaction design at the atomic level. Dan's delivered that in spades."

—*Jared Spool, User Interface Engineering*

"*Microinteractions* is an essential guide to designing in today's world where a typical person touches a hundred different user experiences each day, and only the clearest interactions will turn a new user experience into a cherished product.

"In this book, Dan Saffer turns the Cognitive Walkthrough on its head and takes it to the next level, creating a new model for defining interactions and illustrating the strength of designing for moments rather than systems.

"An easy, jargon-free read and an invaluable reference, *Microinteractions* is packed with vital principles backed up by a wide spectrum of useful real-world examples of what to do and what not to do. You'll get something out of reading any two pages and even more out of reading them again. The book is an example of its own teachings. Approachable, but with deeper insights as needed."

—*Kevin Fox, designer, Gmail*

"Saffer has written an excellent, compact, and eminently readable volume on a subject under-valued and under-discussed in our industry: the art and science of creating small, delightful moments in our daily interactions with technology. I recommend it to any designer or programmer looking to enhance the desirability and polish the utility of their apps, sites, or services, one interaction at a time."

—*Robert Reimann, Founding President, Interaction Design Association (IxDA); Principal Interaction Designer, PatientsLikeMe; co-author, About Face 3 (Wiley)*

Microinteractions

Dan Saffer

O'REILLY®

Beijing · Cambridge · Farnham · Köln · Sebastopol · Tokyo

Microinteractions

by Dan Saffer

Copyright © 2013 Dan Saffer. All rights reserved.

Printed in the United States of America.

Published by O'Reilly Media, Inc., 1005 Gravenstein Highway North, Sebastopol, CA 95472.

O'Reilly books may be purchased for educational, business, or sales promotional use. Online editions are also available for most titles (*http://my.safaribooksonline.com*). For more information, contact our corporate/institutional sales department: 800-998-9938 or *corporate@oreilly.com*.

Editor: Mary Treseler		**Indexer:** Angela Howard	
Production Editor: Rachel Steely		**Cover Designer:** Randy Comer	
Copyeditor: Kiel Van Horn		**Interior Designer:** David Futato	
Proofreader: Rebecca Freed		**Illustrator:** Rebecca Demarest	

May 2013:   First Edition

Revision History for the First Edition:

2013-04-25:   First release

See *http://oreilly.com/catalog/errata.csp?isbn=9781449342685* for release details.

Nutshell Handbook, the Nutshell Handbook logo, and the O'Reilly logo are registered trademarks of O'Reilly Media, Inc. *Microinteractions*, the image of an English sparrow and a tree sparrow, and related trade dress are trademarks of O'Reilly Media, Inc.

Many of the designations used by manufacturers and sellers to distinguish their products are claimed as trademarks. Where those designations appear in this book, and O'Reilly Media, Inc., was aware of a trademark claim, the designations have been printed in caps or initial caps.

While every precaution has been taken in the preparation of this book, the publisher and author assume no responsibility for errors or omissions, or for damages resulting from the use of the information contained herein.

ISBN: 978-1-449-34268-5

[LSI]

Table of Contents

Foreword

I first encountered Dan Saffer's interest in microinteractions at a conference in Brazil. I was immediately captivated. Dan started his talk with the story of the ringing cellphone at a symphony concert that forms the opening pages of Chapter 1. It was very clear that by focusing upon the small, Dan had discovered something very big.

I next encountered the importance of getting the details right through my own frustrations with Apple's photo cataloging and editing application, Aperture. I was putting together the illustrations for a book when suddenly my computer froze and I had to force a reboot. But when I tried to open Aperture, it announced that the database was corrupted and promptly shut down. Huh? What is the use of an error message that provides no remedy? What was I supposed to do?

I searched the Aperture help files. No luck. I searched Apple's support website. No luck. I was annoyed and concerned: *How could I get the photos back?* The program wouldn't even launch. I keep a backup on another computer, but my synchronization program was far too efficient: the corrupted file had been transferred to the other computer.

Finally, after much travail, an Internet search yielded the solution, described in a very nicely formatted set of instructions from Apple. I followed the instructions and 15 minutes later, all my photos were restored. (Note that I couldn't find this from the Apple site: I found a discussion group where someone had posted the link to the proper location at Apple.)

Why am I telling you this? Because if only Apple's programmers had read this book, I wouldn't have had to go through any agony. Microinteraction. Get the details right.

Why didn't that error message contain the solution as well as identifying the problem? After all, Apple had a very nice message explaining the problem and saying just what to do about it. Suppose the error message had said, "The database is corrupted: to correct this, follow these steps" (with active buttons on the message dialog box that would initiate the process). Why didn't Apple do this? Was it because the programmers for this part of the program didn't consider it part of their responsibility? Was it because these programmers came from a different group that maintained the database, so they only knew there was a problem but not how to fix it? Or was it because it is not in the culture of error-message writers to also provide the solution? (My best guess is that all three factors played a role.) Whatever the reason, the result is an inferior user experience, one that now has me extremely unhappy with Aperture, searching for a better alternative. This can't be the response Apple wants to produce in its customers. If only they had been able to read this book.

Are microinteractions details? Damn right: the magic is all in the details.

The "micro" in "microinteractions" implies it is about the small things. Small? Yes. Unimportant? Absolutely not! *Microinteractions* is about those critical details that make the difference between a friendly experience and traumatic anxiety. As Dan Saffer points out in his Preface, designers love to get the big picture right. It's a wonderful feeling. No problem is too large. But even if the big picture is done right, unless the details are also handled properly, the solution fails: the details are what control the moment-to-moment experience. It is timely details that lead to seamless interaction with our products. Alternatively, it is the lack of attention to those details that lead to frustration, irritation, and eventually an intense dislike of the product. Yes, the big picture matters, but so too does the detailed picture. It is attention to detail that creates a smooth feeling of accomplishment.

There are several steps to great microinteractions. The first, and for many developers, the hardest, is to identify the situation properly. This requires great observational skills: watching people interact, watching yourself interact, identifying the pain points, identifying logical sequences, and then determining which things make sense to bring together. Obvious candidates can be found in error messages and dialog boxes. Each presents some information, thus implying the next step to be performed. Why not make that next step part of the present step?

Great microinteraction design requires understanding the people who use the product, what they are trying to accomplish, and the steps they need to take. It requires understanding the context of those interactions. It is essential to develop empathy with the user, to develop the users' observational skills, and to instill the knowledge of how to combine different aspects of your product—perhaps the result of different programming teams or even different divisions—into a single, smooth microinteraction. Chapter 1 does a great job of introducing the principles of how to do this. The numerous examples throughout the book sensitize you to the opportunities that microinteractions provide. After that it is up to you: it is your continual observation that leads to discovery of new microinteraction opportunities. And it is essential not to be blocked, as Apple's developers apparently were, if the solutions require cutting across company organizational structures. After all, doing things right for the user is what great products are all about.

The second step to great microinteraction is the implementation. There are lots of design issues here: triggers, rules, feedback, loops, and modes—all nicely described within the chapters of this book.

Are microinteractions important? Well, let me tell you of my last major purchase: a new automobile. When I walk up to it and put my hand around the door handle, the handles light up and an interior light turns on. The door unlocks, and as I enter the car, the seat, mirrors, and even the programming of the radio resets itself to my preferences. When I open the door, the ceiling light for the seat comes on. If my passenger opens his door, that light comes on. As my wife and I take turns driving, the car resets itself each time to the settings each of us prefers. How did the car designers decide upon this sequence? How did they decide which things to control or not control? By clever, intelligent microdesign. Are these small things? Yes. Could we have manually done all of this? Yes. But when the car does it for us, it provides a sense of delight in the car, a feeling of pride of ownership. Isn't that what all product manufacturers should want for their customers?

Hurrah for the small, which is where we spend most of our lives. Hurrah for those many seconds and minutes spent seeking how to do the next step, the frustrations of inelegant transitions. Hurrah for Dan Saffer and this book, where the friendly writing style is enhanced through copious examples. I considered myself skilled at observing people interacting with technology, but after reading this book, my skills have improved. Now I look more closely at the details, at the missed opportunities. I also see where products do things right. Learning to see is the first step toward making thing better.

Now it is your turn: go out and conquer. Make our lives simpler, more enjoyable. Put microinteraction awareness into practice.

—Don Norman (*don@jnd.org*)
Norman group, Silicon Valley, California
Author of Design of Everyday Things, Revised and Expanded

Preface

What Is This Book About?

Microinteractions are all around us, from the turning on of an appliance to logging in to an online service to getting the weather in a mobile app. They are the single use-case features that do one thing only. They can be stand-alone apps or parts of larger features. The best of them perform with efficiency, humor, style, and an understanding of user needs and goals. The difference between a product we love and a product we just tolerate are often the microinteractions we have with it.

This book dissects microinteractions in order to help readers design their own. Starting with a model of microinteractions, each chapter closely examines each part of the model, and provides guiding principles to get the most out of every microinteraction. By doing so, your products will improve and your users will enjoy using them more, building customer (and brand) loyalty.

Who Should Read This Book

This book is for anyone who cares about making better products, particularly digital products. Designers of all stripes, developers, researchers, product managers, critics, and entrepreneurs will hopefully find much to think about, use, and emulate here.

This book is especially for anyone who has struggled to convince their client, developers, the product or project managers that *this small thing* is really worth doing, that it'll make the product *so much better*. Now that small thing has a name—microinteractions—and can be argued for more effectively.

How This Book Is Organized

This is a small book about a small but important topic.

Chapter 1, Designing Microinteractions

Introduces microinteractions and discusses why something seemingly so insignificant is so important. The structure of microinteractions is discussed, laying out the overall pattern that all microinteractions follow. Lastly, this chapter looks at how microinteractions can be incorporated into projects.

Chapter 2, Triggers

Introduces triggers, the moment that microinteractions begin. Both manual (user-initiated) and system triggers are reviewed. The principle of Bring the Data Forward is discussed.

Chapter 3, Rules

Presents a discussion of rules, the hidden parameters and characteristics that define a microinteraction: how rules are created and what they should encompass, including the principle of Don't Start from Zero.

Chapter 4, Feedback

Discusses feedback, or how the rules are understood by the user. When to use feedback, as well as the three major types of feedback: visual, audio, and haptic. The principles of Thinking Human and Using What Is Often Overlooked are introduced.

Chapter 5, Loops and Modes

Discusses loops and modes, the "meta" parts of microinteractions. The types of modes and loops are discussed, as well as how to use long loops.

Chapter 6, Putting It All Together

Puts together all the pieces of the microinteractions model to design three sample microinteractions: one for a mobile app, another for an online app, and the third for an appliance. This is also where we'll discuss linking microinteractions together to form features.

Appendix A

Touches on the process of testing microinteractions.

Why Write a Book About Microinteractions?

Over the last decade, designers have been encouraged to think big, to solve "wicked problems," to use "design thinking" to tackle massive, systemic issues in business and in government. No problem is too large to not apply the tools of design to, and design engagements can involve everything from organizational restructuring to urban planning.

The results of this refocusing of design efforts are unclear. But by working at such a macro scale, an important part of design is often lost: the details that delight. Products that we love show an attention to detail: the beautiful curve, the satisfying click, the understandable mental model.

This is another way to work: not through grand, top-down design projects, but from the bottom up, by crafting—lovingly, with care—small things. This is something designers can do quite well, with immediate, tangible results. This is another way to change the world: by making seemingly inconsequential moments into instances of pleasure.

There is a joy in tiny things that are beautiful and work well. This joy is both on the part of the user and in the creator, even though it certainly takes skill, time, and thought to make it so. It's hard work, and as admirable in its own way as tackling the Big Problems. After all, who doesn't need more joy in their life?

Conventions Used in This Book

The following typographical convention is used in this book:

Italic
    Indicates new terms, URLs, email addresses, filenames, and file extensions.

 This icon signifies a tip, suggestion, or general note.

 This icon indicates a warning or caution.

Using Code Examples

This book is here to help you get your job done. In general, if this book includes code examples, you may use the code in your programs and documentation. You do not need to contact us for permission unless you're reproducing a significant portion of the code. For example, writing a program that uses several chunks of code from this book does not require permission. Selling or distributing a CD-ROM of examples from O'Reilly books does require permission. Answering a question by citing this book and quoting example code does not require permission. Incorporating a significant amount of example code from this book into your product's documentation does require permission.

We appreciate, but do not require, attribution. An attribution usually includes the title, author, publisher, and ISBN. For example: "*Microinteractions* by Dan Saffer (O'Reilly). Copyright 2013 Dan Saffer, 978-1-449-34268-5."

If you feel your use of code examples falls outside fair use or the permission given above, feel free to contact us at *permissions@oreilly.com*.

Safari® Books Online

Safari Books Online (*www.safaribooksonline.com*) is an on-demand digital library that delivers expert content in both book and video form from the world's leading authors in technology and business.

Technology professionals, software developers, web designers, and business and creative professionals use Safari Books Online as their primary resource for research, problem solving, learning, and certification training.

Safari Books Online offers a range of product mixes and pricing programs for organizations, government agencies, and individuals. Subscribers have access to thousands of books, training videos, and prepublication manuscripts in one fully searchable database from publishers like O'Reilly Media, Prentice Hall Professional, Addison-Wesley Professional, Microsoft Press, Sams, Que, Peachpit Press, Focal Press, Cisco Press, John Wiley & Sons, Syngress, Morgan Kaufmann, IBM Redbooks, Packt, Adobe Press, FT Press, Apress, Manning, New Riders, McGraw-Hill, Jones & Bartlett, Course Technology, and dozens more. For more information about Safari Books Online, please visit us online.

How to Contact Us

Please address comments and questions concerning this book to the publisher:

O'Reilly Media, Inc.
1005 Gravenstein Highway North
Sebastopol, CA 95472
800-998-9938 (in the United States or Canada)
707-829-0515 (international or local)
707-829-0104 (fax)

We have a web page for this book, where we list errata, examples, and any additional information. You can access this page at *http://oreil.ly/Microinteractions*.

To comment or ask technical questions about this book, send email to *bookques tions@oreilly.com*.

For more information about our books, courses, conferences, and news, see our website at *http://www.oreilly.com*.

Find us on Facebook: *http://facebook.com/oreilly*

Follow us on Twitter: *http://twitter.com/oreillymedia*

Watch us on YouTube: *http://www.youtube.com/oreillymedia*

Acknowledgments

I am extremely grateful for Floris Dekker and Andrew McCarthy, the editors and collectors of the tremendous blog Little Big Details, where most of the images in this book are drawn. Without question, I don't think this book would have been written without the examples so readily available to me there. My thanks to them, and particularly to the many contributors to their site. I have tried to credit them whenever I could track down their names.

Jack Moffett, writer of the "Design A Day" blog, should also get a nod of appreciation. Not only did I draw many examples from his "In the Details" section, but how he dissected those details has long been inspirational to me and led indirectly to this book.

My technical reviewers have greatly improved this book with their encouragement, wisdom, and keen eyes: Robert Reimann, Christopher Fahey, Dani Malik, Nick Remis, Dave Hoffer, Bill Scott, and Scott Jenson.

Despite the less-than-stellar performance of my last (before its time) O'Reilly book, I'm grateful for my editor Mary Tresler and everyone at O'Reilly for giving me another shot with this book, and being unfailingly supportive about a small book on a strange topic.

As always, the fortitude of the women (human and canine) I live with cannot be underestimated. This book in particular tested the patience of our house, as I could only write it in the club chair that sits in the middle of our TV room. This book is dedicated to them.

Lastly, a hat tip to the teachers and designers I have worked with and learned from, past and present, who have taught me—sometimes forcibly—the value of focusing on the details. Always, always, it has been some clever little bit they've imagined or have encouraged me to invent that brings the product we're working on to life. It's that spark I hoped to capture here.

—Dan Saffer
San Francisco, February 2013

CHAPTER 1

Designing Microinteractions

"Nothing big works."

—Victor Papanek

The furious shouting started after the conductor stopped the performance. The New York Philharmonic had reached the very end of the slow, quiet Adagio movement that finishes Mahler's Symphony no. 9. The audience, many of whom had paid hundreds of dollars for this privilege, sat attentive and rapt, listening to the still, sublime moments that resolve over an hour of music.

And then it happened: from the front row, the unmistakable sound of an iPhone's "Marimba" sound—that high-pitched xylophone tinkle—going off over and over again. An alarm. It kept going. And going. The conductor, Alan Gilbert, halted the orchestra. But the alarm kept going off. By now, audience members were yelling at the phone's owner, an older executive the Philharmonic later dubbed "Patron X," a long-time symphony patron. Avery Fisher Hall, which just moments before had been unearthly calm and quiet, had erupted in chaos and anger.

As the *New York Times* reported in January 2012,[1] Patron X had just gotten the iPhone the day before; his company had replaced his Blackberry for it. Before the performance began, he had flipped the mute switch, turning silent mode on. But what he didn't know was that one of the iPhone's rules was that alarms still go off even when the phone is silenced. So when the alarm went off, he didn't even realize it was his phone for an excruciatingly long time. By the time he knew it was his phone and had turned the alarm off, it was too late: the performance was ruined.

The next day, as news spread, the Internet exploded with vitriol and wisecracks. Composer Daniel Dorff tweeted, "Changed my ringtone to play #Mahler 9 just in case."

---

1. Daniel J. Wakin, "Ringing Finally Ended, but There's No Button to Stop Shame." *The New York Times*, January 12, 2012.

Arguments and discussions spanned across blogs, with some advocating that turning the ringer off should turn every sound off. In his January 2012 Article "Daring Fireball: On the Behavior of the iPhone Mute Switch" (*http://bit.ly/15n2aOp*) tech columnist Andy Ihnatko wrote, "My philosophy is 'It's much better to be upset with yourself for having done something stupid than to be upset with a device that made the wrong decision on its own initiative.' "

While others made the (in my opinion, correct) case that alarms still need to sound even when the ringer is turned off. As Apple pundit John Gruber pointed out (*http://bit.ly/17wfVHo*), "If the mute switch silenced everything, there'd be thousands of people oversleeping every single day because they went to bed the night before unaware that the phone was still in silent mode."

Apple's own iOS Human Interface Guidelines (*http://bit.ly/YzDKdk*) gives its rationale for why muting the phone works the way it does:

> For example, in a theater users switch their devices to silent to avoid bothering other people in the theater. In this situation, users still want to be able to use apps on their devices, but they don't want to be surprised by sounds they don't expect or explicitly request, such as ringtones or new message sounds.
>
> The Ring/Silent (or Silent) switch does not silence sounds that result from user actions that are solely and explicitly intended to produce sound.

In other words, muting the phone does not silence the sounds that users have specifically asked for, only those they have not (e.g., text messages, incoming phone calls). This is the rule. Like many rules, it's hidden, and it's compounded by the fact that other than the tiny orange mark on the switch, there is no onscreen indicator that the ringer is off. If Apple was to change to a different rule—that the silent switch silences everything—other rules and feedback would have to be designed. Would the phone vibrate when an alarm went off? Would there be some persistent indicator that the phone was in silent mode, either onscreen when you woke up the phone or a small LED indicator in the hardware? There are many different ways silencing a phone could be designed.

Silencing a phone is an example of a microinteraction. A microinteraction is a contained product moment that revolves around a single use case—a tiny piece of functionality that only does one thing (see Figure 1-1 for an example). Microinteractions can power an entire app or device, or (more often) exist alongside or inside a larger product. They are the small moments that can be dull and forgettable, or pleasurable and engaging. Every time you change a setting, sync your data or devices, set an alarm, pick a password, turn on an appliance, log in, set a status message, or favorite or Like something, you are engaging with a microinteraction. They are everywhere: in the devices we carry, the appliances in our house, the apps on our phones and desktops, even embedded in the environments we live and work in.

Figure 1-1. An example of a common microinteraction: signup. The Disqus sign-up form cleverly guesses your name based on your email address. (Courtesy Jakob Skjerning and Little Big Details.)

Microinteractions are the functional, interactive details of a product, and details, as Charles Eames famously said,[2] aren't just the details; they are the design. Details can make engaging with the product easier, more pleasurable—even if we don't consciously remember them. Some microinteractions are practically or literally invisible, and few are the reason that you buy a product; instead, they are usually pieces of features, or the supporting or so-called "hygiene" functionality. For example, no one buys a mobile phone for the ability to turn the ringer off, but it's expected, and, as we've seen, that microinteraction can create all sorts of experiences—for good and bad. Some microinteractions can be frustrating, some dull and forgotten, while the best are engaging and clever. It's this last that this book will provide the tools to design.

The case of Patron X is one of the few examples of a microinteraction making news. Even though we're surrounded by microinteractions every day, we don't usually notice them until something goes horribly wrong, as it did for Patron X. But microinteractions are, despite their small size and near-invisibility, incredibly important. The difference between a product you love and a product you tolerate is often the microinteractions you have with it. They can make our lives easier, more fun, and just more interesting if done well. That's what this book is all about: how to design microinteractions well.

---

2. See *100 Quotes by Charles Eames*, Charles Eames (Eames Office, 2007).

This chapter will teach you how to distinguish microinteractions from features, and gives a brief history of microinteractions. Then, we'll dive into the structure of microinteractions, which also forms the structure of the rest of the book. The microinteractions model will provide a means of discussing and dissecting every piece of a microinteraction so that you can design or improve your own microinteractions. Finally, we'll talk about how to incorporate microinteractions into your process.

Microinteractions Are Not Features ... But Still Matter

The combination of well-designed micro- and macro- (feature) interactions is a powerful one. This is what experience design truly is: paying attention to the details as well as the big picture so that users have a great experience using the product (see Figure 1-2).

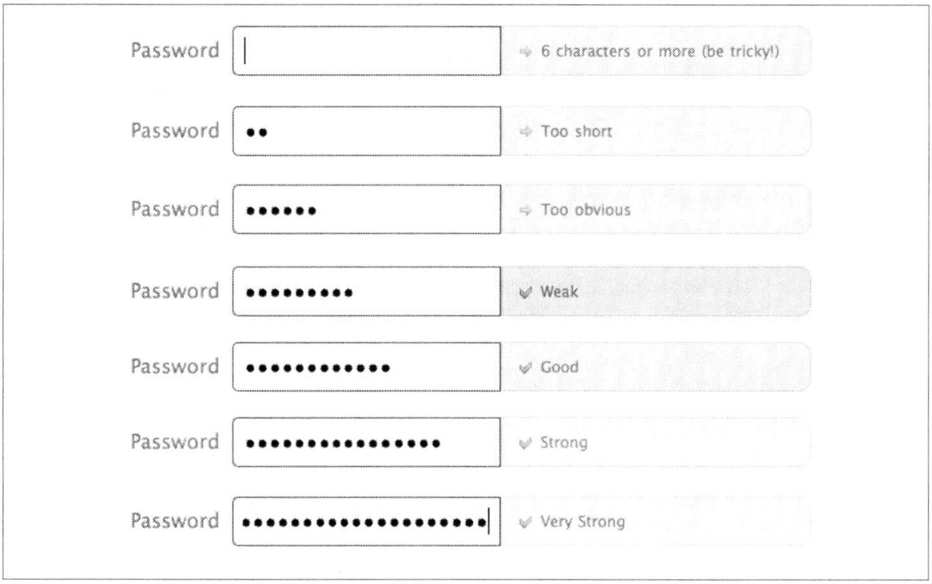

Password		⇢ 6 characters or more (be tricky!)
Password	••	⇢ Too short
Password	••••••	⇢ Too obvious
Password	•••••••••	⩗ Weak
Password	••••••••••••	⩗ Good
Password	••••••••••••••••	⩗ Strong
Password	•••••••••••••••••••••	⩗ Very Strong

Figure 1-2. Twitter's password-selection form is a great variation on a common microinteraction (picking a password), with very clear feedback. (Courtesy Little Big Details.)

Microinteractions differ from features in both their size and scope. Features tend to be complex (multiuse case), time consuming, and cognitively engaging. Microinteractions on the other hand are simple, brief, and should be nearly effortless (see Figure 1-3). A music player is a feature; adjusting the volume is a microinteraction inside that feature.

Microinteractions are good for:

- Accomplishing a single task
- Connecting devices together
- Interacting with a single piece of data, such as a stock price or the temperature
- Controlling an ongoing process, such as changing the TV channel
- Adjusting a setting
- Viewing or creating a small piece of content, like a status message
- Turning a feature or function on or off

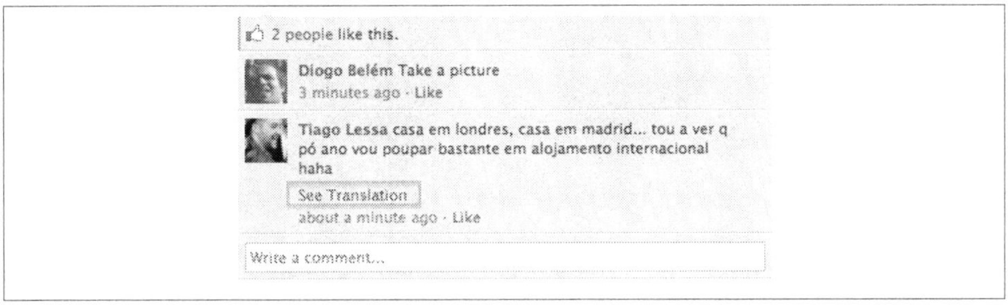

Figure 1-3. When someone posts on your Facebook page in a language that isn't your default, Facebook offers to translate. (Courtesy Marina Janeiko and Little Big Details.)

Microinteractions Can Be Big

Microinteractions can be part of a product—or even the entire product itself. Take a toaster, for example. A toaster does one thing: toasts. It only has one use case: a user puts item to toast into the toaster and presses start. Toaster toasts. Toast pops up when done. That's it. Now, of course, there are variations to this (toasting a bagel instead of bread), but in general the whole device is powered by a single microinteraction.

Similarly, small apps can be made up of one microinteraction. Thousands of small apps —desktop and mobile—do one small thing well, whether it's converting measurements like Convertbot (see Figure 1-4), being a calculator, or showing weather data.

Figure 1-4. Tapbot's Convertbot is an app built around a single microinteraction: converting one value to another.

Microinteractions are frequently the last parts of a product to be designed and developed, and as such they are often overlooked. But ignoring them is a mistake. The reason the original (G1) version of Android felt so unpolished was because the microinteractions were clunky, especially in comparison to the iPhone; for example, deleting items was inconsistently triggered, and in some applications pressing the search key did nothing at all. If the microinteractions are poor, the main features, no matter how nicely done, are surrounded by pain and frustration. The design of your product is only as good as its smallest part.

Consider that almost all operating systems, be they mobile or desktop, do basically the same things: install and launch applications, manage files, connect software to hardware, manage open applications and windows, etc. But the difference between operating systems—at least from a user's perspective—are the microinteractions you have with it on a daily, even hourly, basis (see Figures 1-5 and 1-6).

Figure 1-5. The author's menu bar in OS X is crammed full of icons, each of which launches a microinteraction.

Of course, some features are so useful and/or powerful (or so highly protected by intellectual property laws) that the microinteractions don't matter as much. Many medical devices are examples of this, as is most early stage technology, when people are more amazed something *can* be done rather than *how* it's done. For instance, the first generation of the Roomba (introduced in 2002) couldn't calculate room size or detect obstacles and dirt, but it was a novel technology nonetheless, and subsequent models (especially now that there are competitors on the market) have focused more on the human–robot microinteractions.

Figure 1-6. When trying to find a word on a page, Chrome indicates in the scrollbar where instances of that word appear. (Courtesy Saul Cozens and Little Big Details.)

In competitive markets, microinteractions are even more important. When there is feature parity, it is the experience using the product that increases adoption and brand loyalty. The overall experience of a product relies heavily on its microinteractions. They are the "feel" in look-and-feel. One reason Google+ fell so flat against Facebook was that its microinteractions, such as sorting users into circles, while initially intriguing, quickly became tiresome and gimmicky.

Another reason to pay attention to microinteractions is because they fit so well into our multiplatform existence. Microinteractions are the glue that can tie together features across mobile devices, TV, desktop and laptop computers, appliances, and the Web. While the microinteractions could vary by platform, their small size allows for a consistency that you might not have with large features. In particular, appliances and mobile devices with their small (or no) screens seem custom-made for microinteractions. Small interactions work well on small devices.

Take Twitter for example. Twitter is built entirely around a single microinteraction: sending a <140-character message. Users can do this from practically any device, anywhere. Some objects even tweet independently, or for us. Twitter can be used to send gossip or messages to coordinate a revolution. Well-designed microinteractions can scale well across platforms and to millions of users (see Figure 1-7).

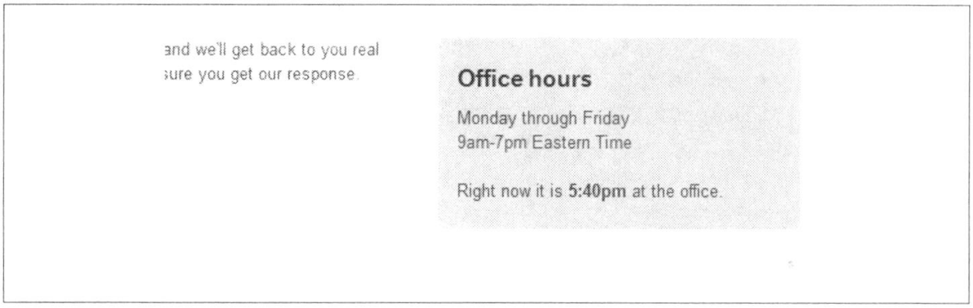

and we'll get back to you real
sure you get our response.

Office hours

Monday through Friday
9am-7pm Eastern Time

Right now it is **5:40pm** at the office.

Figure 1-7. A nice piece of microcopy. When you go to ask for support at Harvest, it shows the time at their office alongside their office hours. (Courtesy Nicolas Bouliane.)

Microinteractions also fit well into our already crowded, overcomplicated, and fragmented lives. We need and even enjoy the fast glance at data, the rapid check-in at a restaurant, the casual review of messages on the subway. (The "Casual Games" category is really a set of stand-alone microinteractions for amusement.)

Microinteractions force designers to work simply, to focus on details. They challenge designers to see how lightweight they can design, to reduce complexity and streamline features that could otherwise be burdensome (Figure 1-8).

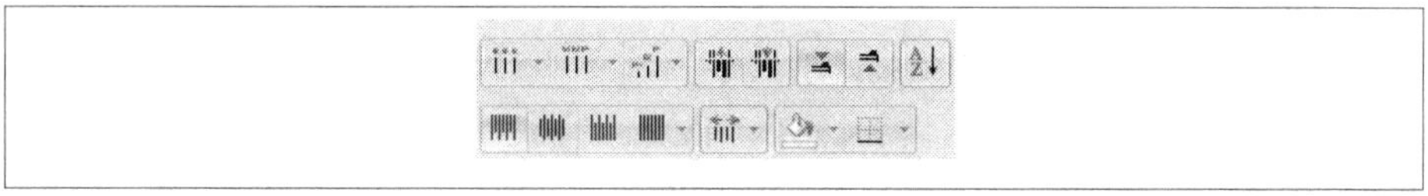

Figure 1-8. In Microsoft Office, when text is rotated, relevant styling buttons are rotated as well. (Courtesy Little Big Details.)

The Secret History of Microinteractions

In 1974, a young engineer named Larry Tesler began working on an application called Gypsy for the Xerox Alto computer. Gypsy was one of the first word-processing applications ever, and the successor to the groundbreaking Bravo, the first true WYSIWYG word-processing program and the first program that could have the ability to change fonts. Even though it was still a word-processing program, Gypsy was a different kind of application altogether: it made use of a mouse and a graphical user interface (GUI). Larry's mission—and what would become his rallying cry for decades to come—was to reduce the modality of the interface, so that users wouldn't have to switch to a separate mode to perform actions. (His website is *http://www.nomodes.com*, his Twitter handle is @nomodes, and even his license plate reads NOMODES (*http://bit.ly/11KzyKV*).) Larry wanted users, when they typed a character key, to always have that character appear onscreen as text—not an unreasonable expectation for a word-processing application. This wasn't the case in Bravo: typing only worked in a particular mode; other times it triggered a function.

One of those functions was moving text from one part of the document to another. In Bravo (see Figure 1-9), users had to first select the destination, then press the "I" or "R" keys to enter Insert or Replace modes, then find and select the text to move, then finally press the Escape key to execute the copy.[3] Larry knew there was a better way to perform this action, so he designed one that not only made use of the mouse, but radically simplified this microinteraction. In Gypsy, the user could select a piece of text, press the "Copy" function key, then select the destination, and finally press the "Paste" function key. No mode required. And thus, cut and paste was born.

The intertwined history of interaction design and human–computer interaction is really the history of microinteractions. The tiny things we unthinkingly interact with every day on desktops, laptops, and mobile devices were once novel microinteractions: everything from saving a document to organizing files into folders to connecting to a WiFi network were all microinteractions that needed to be designed. Even "basics" like scrolling and opening multiple windows needed to be designed and engineered. The forward march of technology has provided a continuous need for new microinteractions. We use them unquestioningly now, and only really pay attention to them when someone designs a better way, or the technology changes and allows for or forces a new way of performing the microinteraction.

---

3. Detailed in *Bravo Course Outline* by Suzan Jerome, published by Xerox, 1976.

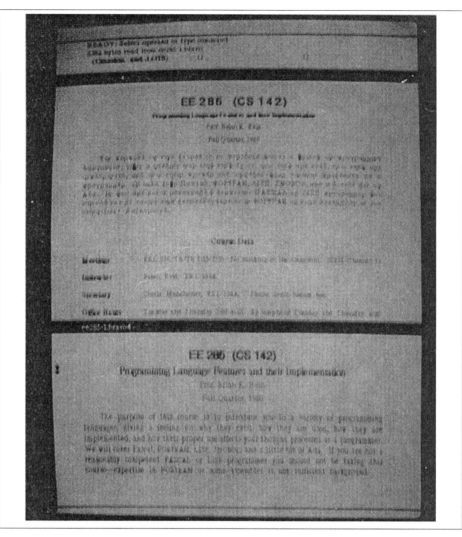

Figure 1-9. A "screenshot" (Polaroid[!]) of Bravo. The bottom window is being used to make a form in the top window. (Courtesy DigiBarn Computer Museum.)

Indeed, as technologies have changed, the microinteractions that support them have also changed. Take scrolling, for instance. Bravo had a primitive version of scrolling, but scrolling really became more refined when Alan Kay, Adele Goldberg, and Dan Ingalls introduced scrollbars in another Xerox PARC product, SmallTalk, sometime between 1973 and 1976. SmallTalk's scrolling could be smooth, pixel-by-pixel, instead of line-by-line. (This was famously one of the UI elements demoed to Steve Jobs and his engineers, which they then built into Apple's Lisa (Figure 1-10)—and subsequently the Macintosh.)[4]

As documents got longer, scrollbars added arrows to jump to the end without scrolling. Tooltip-style indicators would appear to indicate where you were in the document. But the real change came with touchscreen technology on trackpads and mobile devices. Do you slide up or down to scroll down? Apple famously changed directions (from down to up) in OS X Lion after the introduction of its iPhones in order to align its laptops and mobile devices to "natural scrolling." [See, for example, "Apple's Mousetrap: Why did Apple reverse the way we scroll up and down?" by Michael Agger in Slate (*http://slate.me/10nnZN8*).] Apple has also (to the ire of many) hidden scrollbars except when scrolling is in process or the cursor nears the right edge of a scrollable window. The microinteraction keeps evolving.

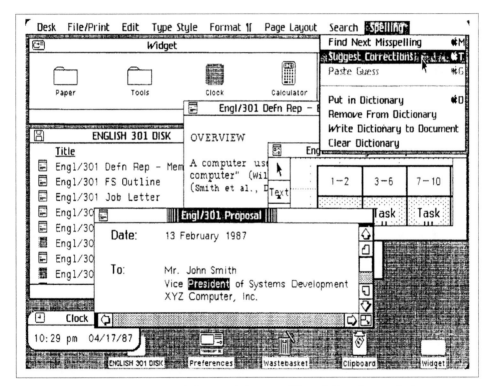

Figure 1-10. Apple's Lisa (1982) featured dozens of "new" (for the market) microinteractions. (Source: Lisa Graphical User Interface Gallery Guidebook.)

4. As recounted in *Dealers of Lightning: Xerox PARC and the Dawn of the Computer Age* by Michael A. Hiltzik (HarperBusiness, 2005).

But it's not just digital products that have microinteractions; a case can be made that microinteractions originated with the first electric devices, such as the radio (1893), the flashlight (1986), and the washing machine (1900). As designer Bill DeRouchey points out in his talk "The History of The Button," in the (pre-electric) mechanical era, users could follow their actions directly from the control to the output. You could pull a lever, watch the gears move and finally see the wheels turn. It was easy to connect the input to the output. Electricity changed all that. You could press a button on the wall and nearly instantly a light on the other side of the room turned on. Sure, the feedback was instant, but the method of execution was not. As DeRouchey says in "The History of the Button" (*http://slidesha.re/1049o1K*), "The button meant for the first time the result of the human motion could be completely different from the motion [it creates] itself." Action became abstracted.

In the digital age, particularly before the GUI, action became even more abstract. Inserting a stack of punchcards or flipping a series of switches produced output that was equally obtuse. For a time, the GUI cleared up and simplified microinteractions. But then Moore's Law (processor speed doubles every 18 months), Koomey's Law (power consumption for hardware decreases 50% every 18 months), Kryder's Law (exponential increase in storage space), and increasing bandwidth and network connectivity (LANs first, then wireless networks, both local and mobile) created the need for more microinteractions, and those microinteractions needed to control actions far more abstract than turning on a light. Just as one example, syncing data across devices is a conceptually abstract idea, for which there's no readily available physical analog.

Input methods are also drastically changing microinteractions. Not only do we have physical controls like buttons, switches, keyboards, and mice, we also have touchscreens, sensors, voice, and gestural means of triggering microinteractions. In the not-too-distant past, the only way to interact with the physical environment was to adjust it manually via a physical control. This changed in 1956 when Robert Adler invented the Zenith Space Commander, the first TV remote control (Figure 1-11). For the first time, users could control an object from a distance, invisibly.

Today, to trigger a microinteraction, you don't even need to be in the same room. With the right equipment, you can adjust the temperature in your house from the other side of the world (see Figure 1-12). Or you only need to be in the right location; just by being in a certain block, your mobile phone can remind you of a to-do item, or your GPS device can tell you where to turn left. In public restrooms, you can turn on sinks just by putting your hands into them. You can tell your phone to find you a nearby restaurant, or flick your finger down a touchscreen list to reveal a search bar, or tap your phone on a counter to pay for your coffee. The list goes on.

The history of technology is also the secret history of the microinteractions that, like symbiotic organisms, live alongside them to frame, manage, and control them.

Figure 1-11. Although there had been remote-control planes and boats previously (mostly for military use), the Space Commander television remote removed proximity from control for consumers. (Courtesy Peter Ha.)

Figure 1-12. The Nest Learning Thermostat uses proximity sensors to know when someone walks into the room, then lights up and shows the temperature in a way that's visible at a glance from across the room. No touching required. (Courtesy of Nest.)

The Structure of Microinteractions

What makes effective microinteractions is not only their contained size, but also their form. A beautifully crafted microinteraction gracefully handles four different parts, which will be described next (see Figure 1-13).

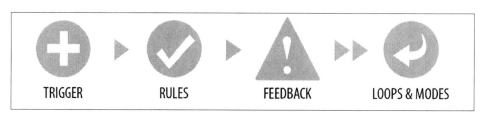

Figure 1-13. The structure of microinteractions.

These four parts—the trigger that initiates the microinteraction, the rules that determine how the microinteraction works, the feedback that illuminates the rules, and loops and modes, the meta rules that affect the microinteraction—are a way to design and dissect microinteractions.

The first part of any microinteraction is the *trigger*. With turning off the ringer on an iPhone, the trigger is user-initiated, meaning that the user has to do something—in this case, flip a switch—to begin the microinteraction. Thus, many microinteractions begin with an understanding of user need: what the user wants to accomplish, when they want to do it, and how often. This determines the affordances, accessibility, and persistence of the trigger. In our silencing-the-phone example, turning off the ringer is a very common action that users want to perform all the time, rapidly. Thus the trigger (the Ringer/Silent switch) is available all the time, instantly able to be turned on and off no matter what application is running. It was so important, it's one of only five physical controls on the iPhone. Controls—digital and/or physical—are the most important part of user-initiated triggers. They provide not only the ability to engage with a microinteraction (and sometimes the ability to adjust it while in progress), but also usually the visual affordance that the microinteraction is even there (see Figure 1-14). If there were no ringer on/off switch on the iPhone, you might expect the phone had that functionality, but have to guess at where to find it. In many older mobile phones (and even in some phones still), silencing the phone was buried under several layers of a settings menu. Even for users who knew where the setting was, it took as much as 10 seconds to turn the ringer on or off. It takes less than a second to flip the physical Ringer/Silent switch.

Of course, the physical control doesn't have to be a switch either. Although the best designs feel inevitable, there is almost nothing designed that could not be designed differently. On Windows Phones, the trigger is a pressable rocker button (which also controls volume) that, when pressed, presents users with a screen overlay that lets users choose ringer status as "vibrate" or "ring + vibrate."

Figure 1-14. An example of a trigger. In iOS (as in Windows Mobile), you can use the camera even on a locked phone. Pressing the camera icon bounces the bottom bar up a little, indicating that you swipe up to get the camera functionality. Of course, slide to unlock is its own trigger as well.

But triggers need not be user-initiated. Increasingly, triggers are system-initiated—when the device or application itself detects that certain conditions have been met and begins a microinteraction. The triggering condition could be anything from detecting that a new email arrived, to the time of day, to the price of a particular stock, to the location of the user in the world. For silencing the phone, one could easily imagine that function integrating with your calendar, so that it automatically silences the phone whenever you're in a meeting. Or by knowing your location, it automatically goes silent whenever you're in a movie theater or symphony hall. As our applications and devices become more sensor-full and context-aware, the more ability they could have to make decisions on their own about how they operate.

Triggers are covered in Chapter 2.

Understandably, users may want, if not the ability to adjust these system-initiated triggers, then at least the understanding of how they operate, just as Patron X probably would have liked to know how silencing his phone worked. In other words, they want to know the *rules* of the microinteraction.

Once a microinteraction has been initiated, it engages a sequence of behavior. In other words: something happens (see Figure 1-15). This usually means turning some piece of functionality or interactivity on, but it might just show the current state of the application or device. It might use data to guess what the user wants to do. In whatever case, it turns on at least one rule, and rules can usually be defined by a designer.

Figure 1-15. An example of a rule. When you're using the music-streaming service Spotify and then turn it on on another platform, the first instance of Spotify pauses. If you resume playing on the first instance, the second platform will pause. This creates a very frictionless, cross-platform service. (Courtesy Sebastian Hall.)

Take what is probably the simplest microinteraction there is: turning on a light. Once you use the trigger (a light switch), the light turns on. In a basic light setup, there is a single rule: the light stays on and fully lit until the switch is turned off. You can change that rule, however, by adding a dimmer or a motion detector that turns the light off when no motion is detected. But the basic turn on switch/turn on light rule is very simple, and one that becomes apparent to anyone who uses a light, even a child.

With applications or electro-digital devices, the rules can be much, much more nuanced and hard to understand, even for small microinteractions. In the case of Patron X, it was the interaction with silencing the phone that caused the symphony incident, because unless there is a specific piece of feedback (and we'll get to that next), rules are themselves invisible. Unlike the mechanical devices of the 19th century, users generally cannot see the activity the trigger has initiated. (This "feature" has been used to tremendous effect by hackers, whose victims launch a program that unbeknownst to them installs a virus onto their computers.)

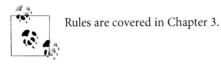

Rules are covered in Chapter 3.

Everything we see or hear while using digital devices is an abstraction. Very few of us really know what's happening when we use any kind of software or device. Just as examples, you're not really putting a "file" into a "folder" and "email" isn't really arriving into your "inbox." Those are all metaphors that allow us to understand the interactions that are going on. Anything you see, hear, or feel that helps you to understand the rules of the system is *feedback*, the third part of microinteractions.

Feedback can take many forms: visual, aural, haptic (vibrations). Sometimes it can be prominent and unmistakable, like the light bulb glowing when you flip the switch. Sometimes it can be subtle and ambient, like the unread badges that appear on email applications and mobile apps. It can be as descriptive as a voice telling you exactly where to turn while doing turn-by-turn directions, or it can be as ambiguous as an LED light blinking in a complicated pattern. It can be as disruptive as the fart-like buzz of your phone in your pocket announcing a message, or a whisper as a digital panel opens. What is important is to match feedback to the action, to convey information in the most appropriate channel possible.

In our turning off the ringer on the iPhone example, silencing the phone has two pieces of feedback: a screen overlay when the switch is turned on or off, and a tiny, visible strip of orange on the actual switch when the phone is silent. What doesn't appear—and what was the downfall of Patron X—is any indication that even though the ringer is off, set alarms will still sound. There is also no onscreen indicator (other than the temporary overlay, which vanishes after a few seconds) that the ringer is off. These are design choices.

Even more than with triggers, feedback is the place to express the personality of the product. Indeed, feedback could be said, along with the overall form, to completely define the product's personality.

Feedback is not only graphics, sounds, and vibrations; it's also animation (see Figure 1-16). How does a microinteraction appear and disappear? What happens when an item moves: how fast does it go? Does the direction it moves in matter?

Figure 1-16. An example of feedback. In Coda2, the Process My Order button becomes a progress bar when pressed. The text should change to Processing Order and Order Processed!, however. (Courtesy Christophe Hermann and Little Big Details.)

Feedback can have its own rules as well, such as when to appear, how to change colors, how to rotate the screen when the user turns a tablet on its side. These rules may themselves become their own microinteractions, as users might want to adjust them manually as a setting.

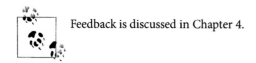 Feedback is discussed in Chapter 4.

The last part of microinteractions are the *loops and modes* that make up its meta rules. What happens over time with the microinteraction: do the interactions remain until manually turned off (as is the case with the Ringer/Silence switch) or do they expire after a while? What happens during an interruption or when conditions change? See Figure 1-17 for an example.

Although it's often undesirable, some microinteractions have different modes. For instance, take the example of a weather app. Its main (default) mode is all about displaying the weather. But perhaps users have to enter another mode to enter the locations they'd like weather data from.

Figure 1-17. An example of a loop. On eBay, if you've bought the same item in the past, the button changes from "Buy it now" to "Buy another." (Courtesy Jason Seney and Little Big Details.)

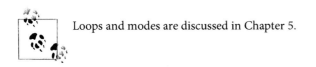 Loops and modes are discussed in Chapter 5.

Microinteractions as a Philosophy

There are three ways of incorporating microinteractions into products. The first is to think about them on a case-by-case basis. During the course of a design project or when simply refining your product, try to identify any possible microinteractions. Make a list of them, then treat each as such. For each one, deliberately consider the structure as outlined in this book, and see if you can polish each individual component. You'll wind up with elegant microinteractions—and possibly *Signature Moments*.

Signature Moments are those microinteractions that are product differentiators. A custom trigger control (such as the original iPod's scroll wheel) or an elegant "loading" animation or a catchy sound ("You've Got Mail!") can be marketed as though they are features and used cross-platform or in other products by the same organization. A Signature Moment will help create customer loyalty and recognition. The Like button on Facebook is now so well known that it's part of the brand.

The challenge in working this way is keeping the scope of the microinteraction limited. The tendency is to turn them into features, because that is the way most designers are used to working. We want to tackle big problems and solve everything. Microinteractions are an exercise in restraint, in doing as much as possible with as little as possible.

Embrace the constraints and focus your attention on doing one thing well. Mies van der Rohe's mantra of "less is more" should be the microinteraction designer's mantra as well.

A second way to think about microinteractions is to reduce more complex applications to individual products that are each built around one microinteraction. This is microinteractions as product strategy: your product does one thing and one thing well. Reduce the product to its essence, its Buddha nature. If you find you want to add another feature to your product, that other feature should be its own product. Many appliances, apps, and devices, including the original iPod, follow this model. This is how many startups work (or at least began), from Instagram to Nest: they did one thing well. The "minimum viable product" can be one microinteraction. Working this way justifies and provokes a radical simplicity to your product, which allows you to say no to feature requests as they arise. Of course, this is also a difficult stance to take, particularly in corporations where the inclination is to sell one product that does everything their customers might need. Imagine breaking up Microsoft Word into individual products! And yet this is what some competitors have done. For example, apps like WriteApp are optimized just for writing, with most of the functionality of a word-processing program stripped away, so that the focus is only on writing, for writers. Evernote began with a simple microinteraction: write notes that are available across platforms.

But there is a third way to think about microinteractions, and that is that most complex digital products, broken down, are made up of dozens, if not hundreds, of microinteractions. You can view a product as the result of all these microinteractions working in harmony. This is what Charles Eames meant when he said the details are the design. Everything's a detail, everything's a microinteraction: a chance to delight, a chance to exceed users' expectations. As Dieter Rams said:

> I have always had a soft spot in my heart for the details. I consider details more important than a great draft. Nothing works without details. Details are the essentials. The standard to measure quality by.[5]

In short, treat every piece of functionality—the entire product—as a set of microinteractions. The beauty of designing products this way is that it mirrors the smaller, more agile way of working that many companies are embracing (Figure 1-18). Of course, the pitfall is that you can get lost in the microinteractions and not see the big picture, that all the details won't fit together into a coherent whole when you're finished. And working this way takes extra time and effort.

---

5. Dieter Rams in conversation with Rido Busse (1980), reprinted in *Design: Dieter Rams &* (1981).

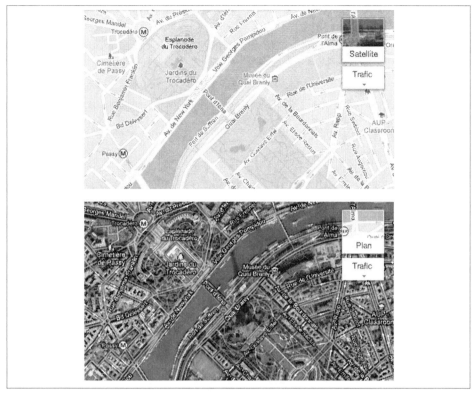

Figure 1-18. Whether viewing the Standard ("Plain") or Satellite view of Google Maps, the widget for changing the view shows the map and a preview of the other view behind it. (Courtesy Hugo Bouquard and Little Big Details.)

This is also a difficult way for agencies—with their notoriously fast project schedules—to work. It's honestly a challenging way for any designer to work, as often the attention of clients and stakeholders is focused on the big features, not the small details that would enhance those features or improve the overall experience. Indeed, it can be difficult to get enough time to focus on microinteractions at all. Convincing business and development team members that microinteractions are worth spending time on can be a challenge. It will likely mean extra time for design and development, after all. But it's worth it.

The disastrous story of Patron X reminds us that microinteractions matter, that the designer's job is to take the tasks that could otherwise be frustrating and difficult and make them otherwise. Larry Tesler knew this when he decided there had to be a better way to move text inside a document, and thus cut and paste were born. Microinteractions can improve the world, one tiny piece at a time. And they all start with a trigger.

Summary

Microinteractions are the small pieces of functionality that are all around us. Focusing on them is the way to create a superior user experience.

The history of microinteractions stretches back to the first electric devices. Most of the digital standards we're used to now were once novel microinteractions.

A microinteraction is made up of four parts: triggers that initiates it, rules that determine how it functions, feedback that the rules generate, and the loops and modes that make up its meta-rules.

There are three ways of working with microinteractions: look for them and focus on each individually, reduce a complicated feature to a core microinteraction, or treat every feature as a set of linked microinteraction.

CHAPTER 2

Triggers

In the 1990s, New York City Transit began converting its seven million daily bus-and-subway passengers from paying fares with tokens—which had been in use since 1904—to paying with a MetroCard, a thin, paper-like plastic card. One of the key pieces of the city's conversion plan was the installation of hundreds of vending machines all over the five boroughs for riders to purchase and fund these new MetroCards. This was no easy task. New York City is home to over eight million people, and tens of millions more live in the surrounding tristate area. According to a report by the Department of City Planning, in 2000, 36% of New York City residents were foreign born; there were enough people speaking a language other than English in 2002 to support 40 magazines and newspapers in another language.[1] Tens of thousands of residents are visually impaired, physically disabled, have little or no schooling, or are illiterate—or some combination

---

1. "Ethnic Press Booms In New York City." *Editor & Publisher.* July 10, 2002.

thereof. The official guide to New York City reports that over 35 million tourists visit every year (in some years as many as 50 million), many of whom will ride the subway, but few of whom are familiar with it or know how to buy a MetroCard. In fact, the Metropolitan Transit Authority (MTA) had done studies of early MetroCard vending machine prototypes and had found that users were intimidated by the physical form and found the user interface to be incomprehensible.

Stepping into this challenge were designers Masamichi Udagawa, Sigi Moeslinger, and their team at Antenna Design, who were tasked with designing the MetroCard Vending Machine.

As Moeslinger recounts,[2] one assumption they had to dispel for themselves was that their users had experience using touchscreen-style kiosks. In the mid-1990s, few people outside of the service industry (where touchscreens were behind bars and fast-food restaurant counters) had much interaction with touchscreens, with one exception: automatic teller machines (ATMs). The designers assumed that even for the lowest common denominator, they would have at least some experience using an ATM. This turned out not to be the case—at the time, anecdotally up to 50% of the MTA riders didn't have a bank account, and thus didn't own an ATM card. They'd likely never used a machine like the MetroCard dispenser. "The concept of a touchscreen was really alien to them," said Moeslinger. Just getting these users—millions of them—to approach and start using the new, unfamiliar machines was a real issue.

Antenna decided to make each screen of the machine only do one task. "It simulates a dialog and asks one question per screen," said Moeslinger. (In other words, they made every screen a microinteraction.) There was some concern by the MTA that by doing so, it would make the transaction too slow. With millions of people using the machines, additional seconds in the transaction could cause lines and rider complaints. But the opposite proved to be the case. "Having quickly graspable bits of information made the transaction much faster than trying to save screens in the steps of the process."

Antenna explored two interaction models: one in which you put your money in first, then you select what you want (like a soda machine) and a second in which you select what you want first, then pay. Users much preferred the second model, but there was still the problem of getting them to start using the new machines in the first place.

Their solution: turn the entire touchscreen into one huge trigger (see Figure 2-1). As discussed in Chapter 1, a trigger is the physical or digital control or condition(s) that begins a microinteraction. In this case the idle screen—the screen that appears after a transaction is completed or when a machine is sitting idle—became a giant call to action: TOUCH ME. As you can see in Figure 2-1, Antenna did everything short of lighting off signal flares to attract users to the trigger. The word "start" appears three times and

2. The full story is told in her 2008 talk "Intervention-Interaction" at Interaction08.

"touch" twice. The hand animates, pointing towards the Start button. But here's the thing: the whole screen is the trigger. You can touch anywhere to begin using the machine. The Start button is just a visual cue—a faux affordance—so that people know to "push" (when they will actually just tap) it to start. Although it seems like the button is the trigger, really it's the whole screen. It's a great solution to a very hard challenge—and one that is still in use over a decade later.

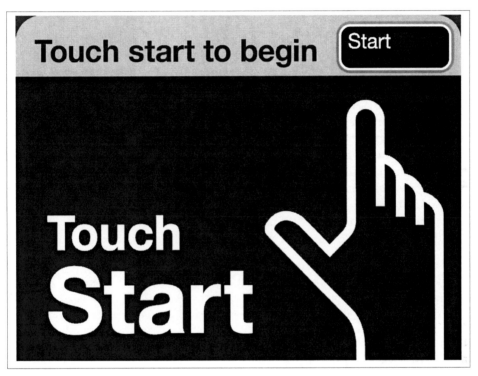

Figure 2-1. The idle screen from the MetroCard Vending Machine. Antenna Design deliberately overemphasized the trigger, which was not, as one might suspect, the button in the top right. It's actually the whole screen. (Courtesy Antenna Design.)

The MetroCard Vending Machine introduces the first principle of triggers: *make the trigger something the target users will recognize as a trigger in context*. This might mean a physical (or seemingly physical, as with the fake Start button on the MetroCard Vending Machine) control like a button or a switch, or it could be an icon in the task or menu bar. Make it look like you can do something, and make it engaging. And while having a large, animated glowing finger pointing up to a Start button isn't the right affordance for most microinteractions, it was appropriate—and wildly successful—for this context.

Manual Triggers

Where do microinteractions begin? Often they are the very first thing a user encounters as they turn a device on or launch an app. The on/off switch (or its digital equivalent) is the first trigger they encounter. On/off switches are, like the Start screen on the MetroCard, examples of manual triggers. (Automatic, system-initiated triggers are covered later.)

Manual triggers usually spring from a user want or need: "I want to turn the TV on." "I want to turn the ringer off on this phone." "I need to move this text from one place to another." "I want to buy a MetroCard." From a strategic point of view, it is critically important to understand what a user wants (or needs) to do, when they want to do it, and in what context(s) they want to do it. This determines when and where your manual trigger should instantiate. It might need to be globally available, like an on/off switch, or it might be very contextual, only appearing when certain conditions are met, such as being in a particular mode or when the user is in a particular functional area of the app. For example, Microsoft Office's "minibar" formatting menu only appears when text has been highlighted. You can find out these user needs the usual ways: either through design research (observations, interviews, exercises) or through intuition and understanding of the subject area. Or you find out the hard way: in product testing or when the product is launched or out in the field. The point is to match the user need (when and where) with the location of the trigger. (See "Making manual triggers discoverable" on page 29.)

The second principle of triggers, although it seems incredible to even have to say this, is *have the trigger initiate the same action every time.* This is so users can create an accurate mental model of how the microinteraction works. This is violated more frequently than one might imagine. Tech reviewer David Pogue on the Samsung S Note:

> Some of the icons in S Note actually display a different menu every other time you tap them. I'm not making this up.[3]

Another example is the Home button on iPhone and iPad, which either takes you to the home screen or, if you're on the home screen, to Search. (Not to mention all the other functions that it does when you press it twice or press and hold. See "Spring-Loaded and One-off Modes" on page 113 in Chapter 5.) While bundling functionality under the home button is a great way to reuse limited hardware, the single press that takes you to Search instead of doing nothing (or giving some kind of "Hey! You're already there!" feedback) if you're on the home screen is probably a step too far.

Possibly the least effective visible triggers are those that are only items in a drop-down menu. As a menu item, the trigger is effectively invisible; if the microinteraction isn't frequently used, having it buried in a menu requires users to do a lot of searching to

---

3. "A Tablet Straining to Do It All" (*http://nyti.ms/17Szx8y*), *The New York Times*, August 15, 2012.

find it. Of course, the alternative is to have a visible trigger onscreen for a microinter-action that is infrequently used, which might not be the best solution either. Settings, such as those for the desktop in Figure 2-2, are a perfect example of this; users only use them infrequently, yet they can be essential for certain apps, so it can be a design challenge to figure out how visible the trigger for them needs to be.

Figure 2-2. On the Gnome desktop, rather than a static text file icon, the icon shows the first three rows of text. (Courtesy Drazen Peric and Little Big Details.)

Bring the Data Forward

The third principle of manual triggers is to *bring the data forward*. The trigger itself can reflect the data contained inside the microinteraction. Ask yourself, what can I show about the internal state of the microinteraction before it is even engaged or while a process is ongoing? What are the most valuable pieces of information I can show? This requires knowing what most people will use the microinteraction for, but you should know that key piece of information before you even begin. A simple example is a stock market app. Perhaps it indicates (via color or an arrow) the current state of the market or a stock portfolio, which could prompt the user to launch the microinteraction—or not. The trigger becomes a piece of ambient information available at a glance that might lead to using the trigger.

The trigger can also indicate where in a process a product is (see Figure 2-3 for an example). The button you use to start a process (making toast, for example) could indicate how long it is until the toast is ready.

Figure 2-3. Google's Chrome browser icon (the trigger to launch it) also indicates active downloads and the download's progress.

The Components of a Trigger

Manual triggers can have three components: the control itself, the states of the control, and any text or iconographic label.

Controls

For manual triggers, the least you can have is a control (see Figure 2-4). The kind of control you choose can be determined by how much control you want to give:

- For a single action (e.g., fast-forward), a button or a simple gesture is a good choice. The "button" in some cases could be an icon or menu item, while the gesture could be a movement like a tap, swipe, or wave. A button could also be (or be paired with) a key command or a gesture.

- For an action with two states (e.g., on or off), a toggle switch makes sense. Alternatively, a toggle button could be used, although it is often hard to tell at a glance what state the button is in—or even that it might have another state. A third (and perhaps worst) choice is that of a regular button where a single press changes the state. If you choose this method, the state the button controls should be absolutely clear. A lamp is clearly on or off, so a regular (nontoggle) button could be used to turn it on and off.

- For an action with several defined states, a dial is a good choice. Aside from having detents, dials can have a push/pull toggle state as well. Alternatively, a set of buttons could be used, one for each choice.

- For an action along a continuum (e.g., adjusting volume) with a defined range, a slide or dial (particularly a jog dial, which can spin quickly) are the best choices. Alternatively, and particularly if there is no defined range, a pair of buttons could be used to change the value up/down or high/low.
- Some manual triggers are made up of multiple controls or elements such as form fields (radio buttons, checkboxes, text-entry fields, etc.). For example, a microinteraction such as logging in might have text-entry fields to put in a username and password. These should be used sparingly and, whenever possible, prepopulated with either previously entered values or smart defaults.

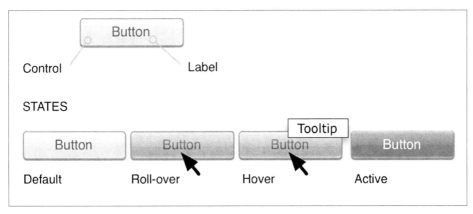

Figure 2-4. The parts of a control.

There are also custom controls that fall outside the traditional buttons, switches, and dials—an example being the scroll wheel from the original (nontouch) iPods. Custom controls will bring a distinct emphasis to your microinteraction, perhaps even making it a Signature Moment. Custom controls can also be gestures or touches (see "Invisible triggers" on page 32).

The goal for microinteractions is to minimize choice and instead provide a smart default and a very limited number of choices. The control you select for the trigger should reflect this philosophy.

Controls are tightly coupled with visual affordances—what users expect can be done, based on sight. The fourth principle of triggers is *don't break the visual affordance*: if your trigger looks like a button, it should work like a button and be able to be pushed.

Making manual triggers discoverable. An important first question to ask is: how noticeable should this trigger be? The fifth principle of triggers is that *the more frequently the microinteraction is used, the more visible it should be.* Author Scott Berkun has a golden rule for discoverability that I've adapted for microinteractions. It's this:

Microinteractions that most people do, most often, should be highly discoverable. Microinteractions that some people do, somewhat often, should be easily discoverable. Microinteractions that few people do, infrequently, should take some searching to find.[4]

This golden rule will serve you well when determining how discoverable your trigger should be.

But how do we discover anything?

There are two ways we as humans become aware of anything in our environment. The first is that the item, either through movement or sound, causes our attention to involuntarily attune to it. This stimulus-driven attention is what kept our ancestors alive, drawing their attention to charging rhinos and other dangers in the environment. Designers can use this same device to draw attention to a trigger by having it move or make noise. Doing this, particularly on a desktop or web environment, can be incredibly obnoxious. Because we involuntarily focus our attention on movement and sound, having a trigger move or make a sound should be reserved for high-priority microinteractions—and to have it repetitively do so should be reserved for the highest priority microinteractions, such as errors and alerts.

The second way we pay attention to anything is when we're actively seeking to find something—when we're goal-based. We actively turn our attention on items/areas to see if we can find something that meets our current needs. This attention, unless we are impaired or blind, is mostly visual. We turn our bodies, heads, or just eyes to visually search for what we're looking for.

 However, it should be noted that our reaction time to sound is faster than visual; auditory stimulus takes 8–10 milliseconds to reach the brain but visual stimulus takes 20–40 milliseconds.[5] Reaction time to sound is also faster: 140–160 milliseconds for sound versus 180–200 milliseconds for visual.[6] Again, this makes evolutionary sense. The human eye is limited to about 180 degrees horizontal and 100 degrees vertical, while hearing is 360 degrees. A predator coming up from behind wouldn't be seen, but could be heard. (Some reptiles and birds actually have 360-degree vision.) But while you could (in theory) use sound as a kind of sonar to find a trigger, in nearly every instance this is impractical.

---

4. Adapted from Scott Berkun, "The Myth of Discoverability" (*http://bit.ly/13uE4NP*).

5. Marshall, W. H., S. A. Talbot, and H. W. Ades. "Cortical response of the anaesthesized cat to gross photic and electrical afferent stimulation." *Journal of Neurophysiology* 6: 1–15. (1943).

6. Welford, A. T. "Choice reaction time: Basic concepts." In A. T. Welford (Ed.), *Reaction Times*. Academic Press, New York, pp. 73–128. (1980).

When we're searching for something, our field of vision can narrow to as little as 1 degree[7] or less than 1% of what we typically see. This narrowing of our field of vision has been compared to a spotlight[8] or zoom-in lens.[9] We engage in a process of object recognition, wherein we identify and categorize items in the environment.

When we're engaged in object recognition, our eyes are looking for familiar shapes, known as geons. Geons are simple shapes such as squares, triangles, cubes, and cylinders that our brains combine together to figure out what an object is.[10]

Because of geons, it's especially good practice to make triggers, particularly iconic ones, geometric. In general, it's easier to find a target when we're looking for a single characteristic rather than a combination of characteristics,[11] so it's best to keep your triggers visually simple—especially if they are going to live in a crowded environment such as among other icons.

Once we identify an item ("That's a button"), we can associate an affordance to it ("I can push a button"), unless there is another visual cue such as it being grayed out or having a big red X over it that negates the affordance. The sixth principle of manual triggers is *don't make a false affordance*. If an item looks like a button, it should act like a button. With microinteractions, the least amount of cognitive effort is the goal. Don't make users guess how a trigger works. Use standard controls as much as possible. As Charles Eames said, "Innovate as a last resort."

The most discoverable triggers are (from most discoverable to least):

- An object that is moving, like a pulsing icon
- An object with an affordance and a label, such as a labeled button
- An object with a label, such as a labeled icon
- An object alone, such as an icon
- A label only, such as a menu item
- Nothing: an invisible trigger

7. Eriksen, C; Hoffman, J. "Temporal and spatial characteristics of selective encoding from visual displays" (*http://bit.ly/11i6pFy*). *Perception & Psychophysics* 12 (2B): 201–204. (1972).

8. Ibid.

9. Eriksen, C; St James, J. "Visual attention within and around the field of focal attention: A zoom lens model." *Perception & Psychophysics* 40 (4): 225–240. (1986).

10. Geons were first espoused in "Recognition-by-components: A theory of human image understanding" by Irving Biederman in *Psychological Review* 94 (2): 115–47. (1987).

11. Treisman, A. "Features and objects in visual processing." *Scientific American*, 255, 114B–125. (1986).

Invisible triggers. Manual triggers can also be invisible—there might be no label or affordance to let the user know there's a microinteraction to be triggered. Invisible triggers are often sensor-based, made possible via touchscreens, cameras, microphones, and other sensors such as accelerometers (as in Figure 2-5). However, you could also have an invisible trigger that is only a command key (Figure 2-6) or a mouse movement (to the corner of the screen, for example).

Figure 2-5. Swiping the button to the left on the Tumblr iPhone app (instead of pressing it) is an invisible trigger for creating a new text blog post. You can also swipe upwards to make a new photo post. (Courtesy Robin van't Slot and Little Big Details.)

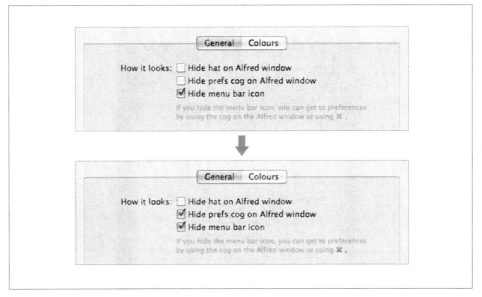

Figure 2-6. In Alfred's settings, if you disable the visible triggers, the invisible one becomes highlighted. (Courtesy Hans Petter Eikemo and Little Big Details.)

Touchscreen UIs currently contain the most common invisible controls. Many multi-touch gestures have no visual affordance to indicate their presence, and custom gestures beyond the usual taps and swipes are often found through a process of trial and error (see Figure 2-7).

Voice input is another example of an invisible control. There are three kinds of voice controls:

Always listening
> The product's microphone is always on and users only need to address it (usually by name) to issue a command. Microsoft's Kinect for Xbox works in this manner. "Xbox, play!" is an example of this kind of control.

Dialogue
> The product's microphone turns on at specific times to listen for a response to a prompt. ("Say 'yes' to continue in English.") Most automated customer call interfaces work thus.

Combined with a control
> In order to initiate a voice command, a physical control has to be engaged first. Apple's Siri works like this: users press and hold the Home button in order to issue voice commands.

Gestural controls such as hand waves to turn something on, or a shake to shuffle are also often invisible. Like voice controls, sometimes there is an initial action (like a wave)

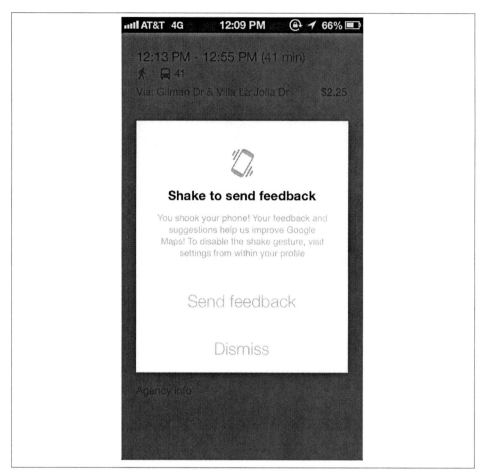

Figure 2-7. In Google Maps for iOS, shaking is an invisible trigger for sending feedback. (Courtesy Little Big Details.)

or a physical control to get the device ready for other gestural commands. With Google Glass, tilting your head upwards or touching the side of the frame turns on the screen. Touching or being close to a device can be an invisible trigger, such as turning on a bathroom sink when hands are put under the faucet. Similarly, moving away from an object can be a trigger as well, such as automatically flushing a toilet when the person has moved away.

Why ever have an invisible trigger? The truth is, no matter what the interface, not every item is going to be immediately discoverable. Making everything visible and discoverable will often mean an incredibly cluttered, complicated, and not easily scannable screen. Hiding items makes the screen or object visually simpler, while not jettisoning functionality (Figure 2-8). Invisible controls allow for an emphasis on what *is* visible, and creates a hierarchy of what's important. But it is important to note that invisibility should not be an explicit goal for microinteraction (or any kind of interaction) design; rather it should be a byproduct of context and technology: what makes sense to hide, given this environment? Or what must we hide because there is no place to display a visible control with this technology? The best microinteractions have just enough interface, but no more.

Figure 2-8. Akismet has a clever invisible trigger. When someone right-clicks the logo (presumably to save it), Akismet shows a window with several different resolutions. (Courtesy Fabian Beiner.)

Invisible triggers should be learnable. Once discovered (either through accident, word-of-mouth, or help), users often only have their (faulty) memories to rely on to initiate the microinteraction again. Being learnable means the invisible trigger should be nearly universally available, or alternatively, only available under particular conditions (Figure 2-9). Invisible triggers should be guessable, or, ideally, stumbled upon as the user performs other actions. For example, scrolling up past the top of a list reveals a reload microinteraction.

Figure 2-9. KanaSwirl's settings allow for disabling what would otherwise be an invisible trigger (Shake to Pause). (Courtesy Shawn M. Moore and Little Big Details.)

Unless it's impossible—there is no screen or place to put a physical control, such as with Google Glass—never make an invisible trigger for a high-priority microinteraction. Try to, at least, create a visible trigger for the microinteraction. For example, a command key and menu items.

Control states

Some manual triggers have multiple states. Although in most cases you won't have all of these states, when designing a trigger, you should consider them:

Default
> The idle state when there is no activity.

Active
> If there is an activity working in the background—for example, downloading an update or syncing—the trigger could be used to indicate that.

Hover
> Can be used to bring up a tool-tip-style description, expand the size of the trigger to reveal more controls or form fields, or simply indicate that an item is clickable. Even more useful, a hover can display a piece of data that is contained within the microinteraction (see Figure 2-10). For example, hovering over an icon that launches a weather app could show you today's weather without ever having to launch the app. Bring the data forward.

Figure 2-10. In the Rdio player, hovering over the fast-forward and rewind buttons display the upcoming or previous track. (Courtesy Nicholas Kreidberg and Little Big Details.)

Rollover
> Often used to indicate presence or activity, or just an added indicator that the cursor is positioned correctly to engage (see Figure 2-11).

On click/tap/in process
> What happens when the trigger is clicked, tapped, or begun. This can mean the trigger disappears, opens, changes color, or becomes a progress indicator as the microinteraction loads (see Figures 2-12 and 2-14). One variation is that the trigger does not launch the microinteraction immediately, but expands the trigger to reveal more controls. For example, a Save button could open up a panel that asks whether to Overwrite or Save As.

Toggle
> Switches and buttons can indicate their current setting (left/right, up/down, or pressed/unpressed, respectively). On physical devices, switches often make this

Figure 2-11. If you aren't logged in and roll over the Comment field, YouTube prompts you to sign in or sign up. (Courtesy Marian Buhnici and Little Big Details.)

Figure 2-12. Path's Sign Up button smiles when clicked. (Courtesy Little Big Details.)

easier to determine this at a glance, unless the button has some accompanying indicator, such as an LED that glows when in a pressed state.

Setting

Dials, switches, and sliders can show what setting or stage the microinteraction is currently at (see Figure 2-13).

These indicators of state are usually the trigger itself—the trigger changes its appearance or animates—but it can also be an indicator light such as an LED positioned near the trigger. For example, a glowing red LED near an on/off switch could indicate its off setting. It's good practice to keep any state indicator that isn't attached to the trigger near the trigger. The same applies for any "expanded" version of the trigger: don't open up a window elsewhere. Keep the focus on the trigger itself.

Figure 2-13. The play/pause control on Xiami.com indicates the playing time of a song. (Courtesy Little Big Details.)

Figure 2-14. In CloudApp, the Log In button changes state after being clicked to let users know an action is happening in the background. (Courtesy Little Big Details.)

Labels

An important part of some triggers are their labels. Labels can name the whole micro-interaction (e.g., the menu item or Microsoft Ribbon item name) or they can be indicators of state, such as a name at each detent on a dial. Labels are interface.

The purpose of a label is clarity: is what I'm about to do the thing I want to be doing? Labels put a name on an action and create understanding where there could otherwise be ambiguity. But because a label becomes one more item to scan and parse, only provide a label if there could be ambiguity. The better practice is to design the control so it has no inherent ambiguity (Figure 2-15).

Figure 2-15. Vimeo's cancel/dismiss/not now button is humorously labeled "I hate change." (Courtesy Joe Ortenzi and Little Big Details.)

The seventh principle of manual triggers is to *add a label only if it provides information that the trigger itself cannot.* Consider how you could represent the label visually instead of by adding text. For instance, imagine a rating system of 1–5 stars. You could design a slider with numeric labels of 1–5 or you could have the trigger be just the five stars that light up one by one on hover.

This is obviously not possible or desirable in some cases. A missing label on a button can mean that that button is indistinguishable from every other button around it and thus is never pushed.

Unlike other kinds of product copy (i.e., instructional, marketing), microinteraction labels are not typically the place for brand creativity; they are utilitarian, to create clarity (see Figures 2-16 and 2-17). This is not to say to ignore whimsy or personality, but to do so only when the label remains clear. Google's "I'm Feeling Lucky" button label might be amusing, but tells you absolutely nothing about what is going to happen when you press the button. There is no feedforward—an understanding of what is going to happen before it happens.[12]

---

12. For more on feedforward, see "But how, Donald, tell us how?: On the creation of meaning in interaction design through feedforward and inherent feedback," by Tom Djajadiningrat, Kees Overbeeke, and Stephan Wensveen, *Proceedings of the 4th conference on Designing interactive systems: processes, practices, methods, and techniques*, ACM, New York, NY, USA (2002).

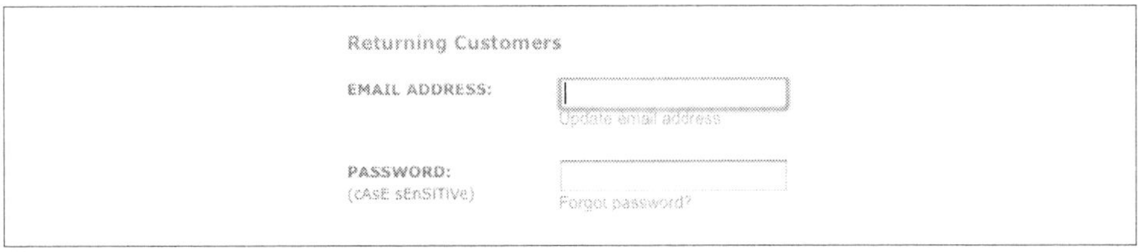

Figure 2-16. Barnes & Noble's website has a label that visually indicates case sensitivity. (Courtesy Paul Clip and Little Big Details.)

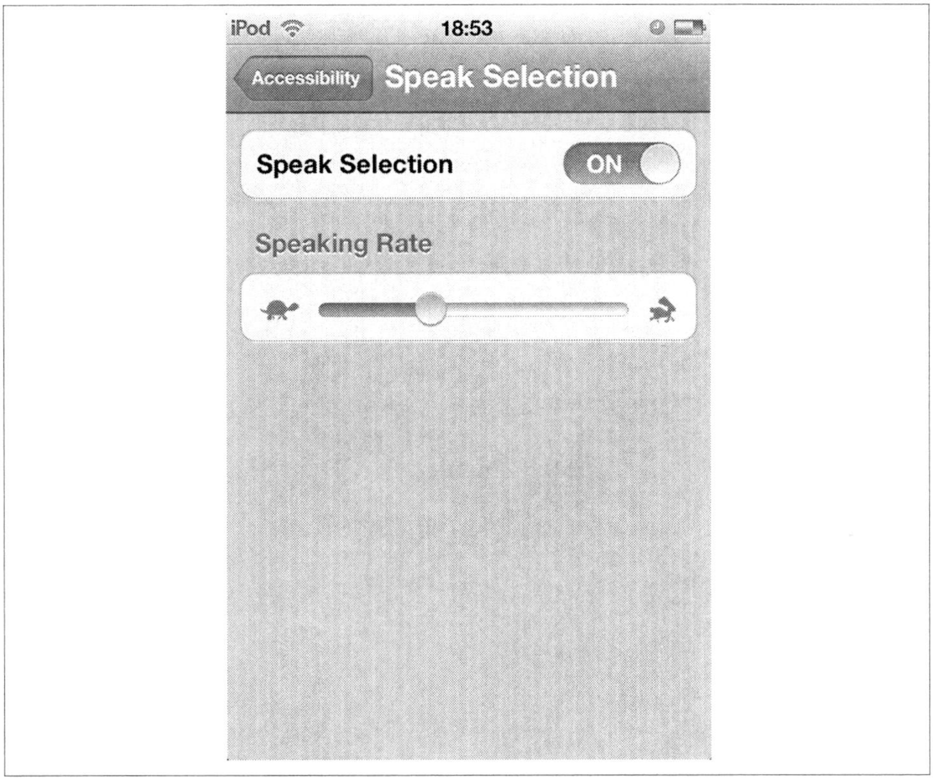

Figure 2-17. Apple's iOS Speak Selection setting has an example of a whimsical but clear iconic label, using the fable of "The Tortoise and the Hare." Although, in cultures where this analogy is unknown, this would certainly be puzzling. (Courtesy Victor Boaretto and Little Big Details.)

In general, labels need to be short yet descriptive and in clear language (Figure 2-18). "Submit" as a button label may be short, but it doesn't clearly indicate in nontechnical language what action the user is about to take. In microinteractions, specificity matters.

Being vague is the enemy of a good label. Be specific. (For more on this topic, see Microcopy in Chapter 3.)

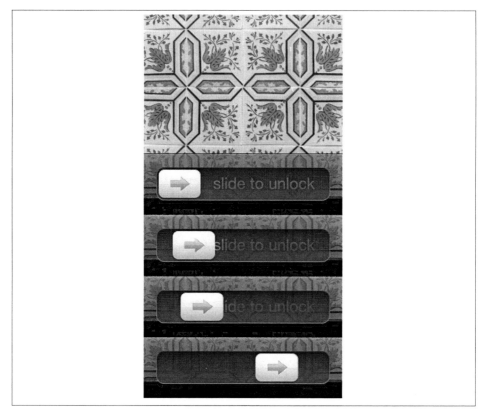

Figure 2-18. The label on the iPhone's Slide to Unlock Trigger vanishes as you slide. (Courtesy Little Big Details.)

Consistency is also important. Since labels can be names, be sure you title anything you're labeling (the microinteraction, a state, a setting, a piece of data) the same name throughout the microinteraction. Don't call it an "alert" in one part of the microinteraction and a "warning" in another part.

The best way to ensure that your labels are successful is to write them in the language of those who will use it. If you're using technical terms, your audience had best be technical as well; otherwise, use casual, plain language. Secondly, test the labels with the target users (see Appendix A). It's not an exaggeration that a majority of usability problems are caused by poor (or no) labeling.

System Triggers

Not all triggers are manual. In fact, we're likely in the era when most triggers aren't human initiated at all, but instead are system initiated. System triggers are those that engage when certain condition(s) are met without any conscious intervention by the user, as in Figures 2-19 and 2-20.

Figure 2-19. The deliveries app checks if there is a tracking number in the clipboard on launch, and if so, a system trigger launches this microinteraction. It's also smart enough to indicate from which courier the number is from. (Courtesy Patrick Patience and Little Big Details.)

Figure 2-20. An example of a system trigger caused by another person. When someone you follow re-blogs someone you don't on Tumblr, a follow button appears. (Courtesy Brian Jacobs and Little Big Details.)

These common conditions that can initiate a trigger:

Errors
    When a system encounters an error, it often addresses the problem via a microinteraction, such as asking what to do or simply indicating something untoward has happened (see Figure 2-21).

Location
    Location can be on many scales: from within a country, to a particular city or neighborhood, to a particular part of a room. A user in any of these settings can cause a microinteraction to fire.

Incoming data
    Email, status messages, software updates, weather, brightness, and a host of other data that enter networked devices and apps can be triggers for microinteractions such as "You've Got Mail!" alerts.

Internal data
    Likewise internal data such as time and system resources can be triggers (see Figure 2-22). An example is dimming the screen after a set amount of time.

Other microinteractions
    One particular kind of system trigger is when one microinteraction triggers another. A simple example of this is a wizard-style interface. The end of step one (a microinteraction) is the trigger for step two (another microinteraction), and so on. (See "Orchestrating Microinteractions" on page 137 in Chapter 6)

Other people
    In many social interactions, what another person does (e.g., reply to a chat, post a picture or message, send a friend request) can be the basis for a trigger.

Figure 2-21. In Windows Phone, the messaging icon (a trigger) changes to a sad face if there was an error sending a message. (Courtesy Wojtek Siudzinski and Little Big Details.)

Password:		USA

Leave Message   Switch User   Cancel   Unlock

Figure 2-22. In Ubuntu, if the screen has timed out and locked, another trigger appears that lets a visitor leave a message for the device's owner. (Courtesy Herman Koos Scheele and Little Big Details.)

Users might not manually initiate these triggers, but it is good practice to provide some means (e.g., a setting) of adjusting them. Every system-initiated trigger should have some manual means of managing or disabling them. Ideally, this is at the point of instantiation, when the microinteraction has been triggered ("Stop showing me these alerts"), but at a minimum in a settings area.

Additionally, users may want a manual control even when there is a system trigger (See Figure 2-23). For example, a user might want to manually sync a document instead of waiting for it to automatically happen. A manual control can provide assurance, as well as the ability to trigger the microinteraction in case there is something wrong with the system (e.g., the network connection is down, or the sensor didn't register).

Figure 2-23. In the Instapaper iPhone app, if you accidentally rotate the phone between portrait and landscape mode and then quickly rotate it back, the Rotation lock setting appears. (Courtesy Richard Harrison and Little Big Details.)

System Trigger Rules

Some system triggers themselves need their own rules, the most common of which are when and how often to initiate (Figure 2-24). It can be system-resource intensive—draining battery life, or using bandwidth or processing power—for a product to be constantly pinging remote servers or reading data from sensors.

System trigger rules should answer the following questions:

- How frequently should this trigger initiate?
- What data about the user is already known? How could that be used to make this trigger more effective, more pleasurable, or more customized? For example, knowing it is the middle of the night could reduce the number of times the system trigger initiates. (See "Don't Start from Zero" on page 64 in Chapter 3 for more.)

- Is there any indicator the trigger has initiated? Is there a visible state change while this is happening? After it's happened? When it is about to happen?
- What happens when there is a system error (e.g., no network connection, no data available)? Stop trying, or try again? If the latter, what is the delay until trying again? (Loops are covered more thoroughly in Chapter 5.)

System trigger rules are closely related to the overall rules, which are covered next in Chapter 3.

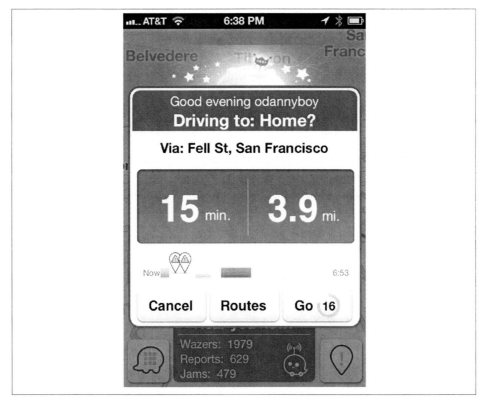

Figure 2-24. Navigation app Waze knows when I open the app in the late afternoon, I'm probably driving home and presents this as an option.

The best triggers are those that, like the Start screen on the MetroCard Vending Machine, fit the context of use and the people who'll use it. The trigger's control matches the states it has to communicate and is appropriately discoverable for how often it will be used. Its labels are clear and written in casual language. And most importantly, it launches users into the actual interaction—the rules.

Summary

A trigger is whatever initiates a microinteraction. Manual triggers are user initiated, and can be a control, an icon, a form, or a voice, touch, or gestural command. System-initiated triggers happen when a certain set of conditions are met.

Make the trigger something the user will recognize as a trigger in context. Have the trigger perform the same action every time.

Bring the data forward. Show essential information from inside the microinteraction on the trigger when possible, such as unread messages or ongoing processes.

If the trigger looks like a button, it should act like a button. Don't break visual affordances.

The more used a microinteraction is, the more visible the trigger should be. Inside a menu is the least visible place for a trigger.

Add labels when there is a need for clarity, when the trigger alone cannot convey all the necessary information. Labels should be brief and in clear language.

System triggers need rules for defining when and how often they appear.

CHAPTER 3

Rules

In October of 2010 at Apple's "Back to the Mac" event, Apple announced the then-latest version of its desktop operating system, Mac OS X Lion (version 10.7), which was released nine months later in July 2011. It sold one million copies on its first day, and over six million copies afterwards. In it, Apple unveiled new versions of Calendar, Mail, and Address Book apps. But there was one microinteraction that garnered a lot of attention, mostly because Apple deemed it unnecessary and removed it. That microinteraction? Save As.

In the early 1980s, Save used to be Save and Put Away (Xerox Star), or Save and Continue alongside Save and Put Away (Apple Lisa). (Put Away meaning close.) Save and Continue eventually just became Save, while Save and Put Away vanished, probably once more RAM allowed for multiple documents to be open at the same time without processor issues. Save As seems to have begun in the 1980s as Save a Copy as, which let users save a version as a new file without renaming. Eventually some applications had all three: Save, Save As, and Save a Copy as. Over time, as people understood the Save As paradigm, and with the broad adoption of the Undo command, Save a Copy as has mostly vanished.

At the time Apple decided to get rid of Save As, the rules of the microinteraction had been fairly stable for about 30 years:

- Make changes to a file.
- Save the file with a new name.
- Subsequent changes happen to the newly created file. The previous file remains as it was the last time it was saved.

With Lion, Apple seemed to feel that Autosave, which allows users to return to previous versions, would obviate the need for Save As. Lion's rules for saving go something like this:

- Make changes to a file.
- Those changes are autosaved every five minutes.
- Subsequent changes happen to the latest version of the file.
- You can rewind to earlier version of the file using the Revert to Last command.
- You can also Browse All Versions, which triggers another microinteraction: the versions browser.
- After two weeks, the file becomes locked and no changes can be made to it without first unlocking it or duplicating it.

If you want to create a separate file, you have to access Duplicate, an entirely different microinteraction:

- Use the Duplicate command to make another (cloned) file.
- The new file appears alongside the current file.

- Rename the new (duplicated) file.
- Subsequent changes happen to the newly created file. The previous file remains as it was the last time it was (auto)saved.

The new rules were practically the inverse of the previous rules: users had to decide *before they made changes* if they wanted the changes to be in a different file. Unfortunately, this is not how most people work (or, more precisely, not how we've been trained to work over the last 30 years). This change severely broke an established mental model and replaced it, not with a better microinteraction but with two microinteractions that together were difficult to understand and misaligned with how most users work. Most people don't need the previous version of their document open at the same time as the altered version. Versioning is what programmers do, not what most people do. When users (infrequently) need an earlier version of a document, they'll manually open it.

Response to the change ranged from puzzlement to outright anger: "The elimination of the Save As... command in applications such as Pages '09 and TextEdit is, in my view, a downright stupid move. It completely breaks a very common workflow for creating a new file, which consists of opening an existing file and saving it under a new name," fumed Macintosh blogger Pierre Igot in "Mac OS X 10.7 (Lion): Why ditch the 'Save As' command?" (*http://bit.ly/11rqVSM*). "I really tried to make myself believe that was an OK decision, but after several months, it was clear that it wasn't," wrote web developer Chris Shiflett in his article "Apple botches 'Save As'" (*http://bit.ly/10nsnf0*).

Apple responded by quietly returning Save As in the 10.8 version of their OS, Mountain Lion, in 2012—although not to the menu, it should be noted, but as a hidden command —an invisible trigger. But it still didn't work as before: the rules changed again. Lloyd Chambers, author of the *Mac Performance Guide (http://macperformanceguide.com/)*, summed up the changes and problems in "OS X Mountain Lion: Data Loss via 'Save As'" (*http://bit.ly/13mpUOU*):

> If one edits a document, then chooses Save As, then BOTH the edited original document and the copy are saved, thus not only saving a new copy, but silently saving the original with the same changes, thus overwriting the original. If you notice this auto-whack, you can "Revert To" the older version (manually), but if you don't notice, then at some later date you'll be in for a confusing surprise. And maybe an OMG-what-happened (consider a customer invoice that was overwritten).

So in Mountain Lion, the rules for Save As work like this:

- Make changes to a file.
- Save the file with a new name.

- Subsequent changes happen to the newly created file. Any changes made to the original file are also saved.

- You can rewind to an earlier version of the original file using the "Revert to Last" command.

This is in addition to the rules for Saving and Duplicating above. So a simple, well-understood microinteraction was replaced by three difficult-to-understand microinteractions, with no feedback as to what the rules are doing in the background. Finally, in an update to Mountain Lion, Apple added a "Keep changes in original document" checkbox in the Save dialog. What a mess.

There are some lessons to be learned. If you can't easily write out or diagram the rules of a microinteraction, users are going to have difficulty figuring out the mental model of the microinteraction, unless you provide feedback to create a "false" model that nonetheless allows users to figure out what is going on. Secondly, unless it's radically new, users likely come to a microinteraction with a set of expectations about how it will work. You can violate those expectations (and in fact the best microinteractions do so by offering an unexpected moment of delight, often by subverting those very expectations), but only if the microinteraction is offering something *significantly better*, where the value to the user is apparent—and, ideally, instantly apparent. Apple is often amazing at this: just as one example, changing the iOS keyboard based on context, so that @ symbols are available on the main keyboard when filling in an email address field. But if the value isn't instantly apparent, your microinteraction could come off as needlessly different, a gimmick. "Things which are different in order simply to be different are seldom better, but that which is made to be better is almost always different," said Dieter Rams.[1]

Designing Rules

At the heart of every microinteraction—just as at the center of every game—are a set of rules that govern how the microinteraction can be used ("played"). What you're trying to create with rules is a simplified, nontechnical model of how the microinteraction operates.

Perhaps the most important part of the rules is the goal. Before designing the rules, you need to determine in the simplest, clearest terms what the goal of the microinteraction is. The best goals are those that are understandable (I know why I'm doing this) and

---

1. Supposedly said in 1993, and quoted by Klaus Kemp in *Dieter Rams: As Little Design as Possible*, Phaidon Press, 2011. Rams may have unknowingly been paraphrasing 18th century German philosopher Georg Christoph Lichtenberg, who said, "Ich weiss nicht, ob es besser wird, wenn es anders wird. Aber es muss anders werden, wenn es besser werden soll." ("I do not know if it is better if it is different. But it has to be different if it is to be better.")

achievable (I know I can do this). Make sure the goal you're defining isn't just a step in the process; it's the end state. For example, the goal of a login microinteraction isn't to get users to enter their password; the goal is to get them logged in and into the application. The more the microinteraction is focused on the goal rather than the steps, the more successful the microinteraction is likely to be. The goal is the engine of the rules; everything must be in service toward it (Figure 3-1).

Figure 3-1. The goal of this microinteraction on Amazon is to prevent users from buying something off their wish list that someone may have purchased already—to prevent a situation...without spoiling the surprise (sort of). (Courtesy Artur Pokusin and Little Big Details.)

While the purpose of rules is to limit user actions, it's important that the rules not feel like, well, rules. Users shouldn't feel like they have to follow—or worse, memorize—a strict set of instructions to achieve the goal. Instead, what you're striving for is a feeling of naturalness, an inevitability, a flow. The rules should gently guide users through the "interaction" of the microinteraction (Figure 3-2).

The rules determine:

- *How the microinteraction responds to the trigger being activated.* What happens when the icon is clicked? (See "Don't Start from Zero" on page 64 later in the chapter.)

- *What control the user has (if any) over a microinteraction in process.* Can the user cancel a download, change the volume, or manually initiate what is usually an automatic process like checking for email?

- *The sequence in which actions take place and the timing thereof.* For example, before the Search button becomes active, users have to enter text into the search field.

- *What data is being used and from where.* Does the microinteraction rely on geolocation? The weather? The time of day? A stock price? And if so, where is this information coming from?

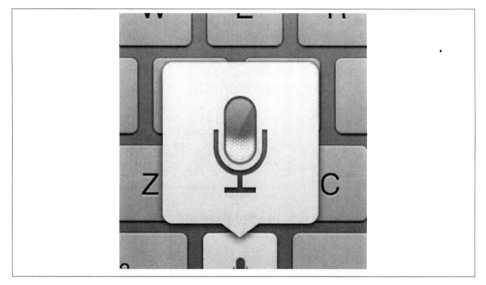

Figure 3-2. In Apple's Mountain Lion OS, when you turn on Speech and Dictation, the fans in the machine slow down so the background noise doesn't interfere. (Courtesy Artur Pokusin and Little Big Details.)

- *The configuration and parameters of any algorithms.* While the rules in their entirety can be thought of algorithmically, often certain parts of a microinteraction are driven by algorithms. (See the section on "Algorithms" on page 78 later in the chapter.)

- *What feedback is delivered and when.* The rules could indicate which "steps" should get feedback and which operate behind the scenes.

- *What mode the microinteraction is in.* A mode is a fork in the rules that, when possible, should be avoided. But sometimes it's necessary. For example, in many weather apps, entering the cities you want to know the weather for is a separate entry mode from the default mode of viewing the weather. See Chapter 5 for more on modes.

- *If the microinteraction repeats and how often.* Is the microinteraction a one-time activity, or does it loop? See Chapter 5 for more on loops.

- *What happens when the microinteraction ends.* Does the microinteraction switch to another microinteraction? Does it vanish? Or does it never end?

The set of rules may or may not be entirely known to the user, and they reveal themselves in two ways: by what can be done and by what cannot (see Figure 3-3). Both of these can be an occasion for feedback (see Chapter 4), although as the story of Patron X in

Chapter 1 demonstrates, sometimes the user's mental model does not match up with the conceptual model that the rules create.

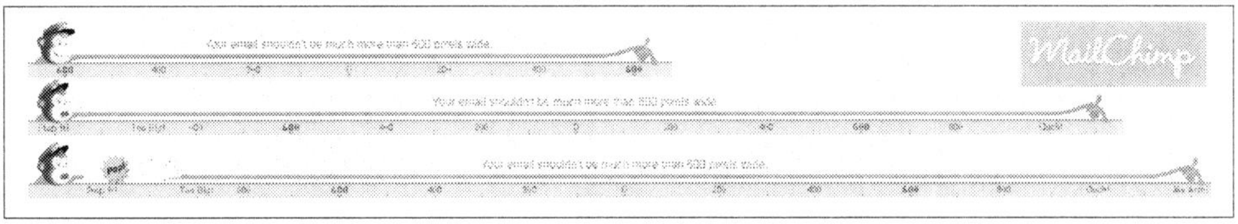

Figure 3-3. MailChimp shows you what can't be done, by having the poor chimp's arm stretch so far that it pops off when you try to make an email too wide. (Courtesy Little Big Details.)

Let's take perhaps the simplest microinteraction there is: turning on a light. The rules are these:

- When the switch is thrown, the light turns on and stays on.
- If the switch is thrown again, turn the light off.

Very simple.[2] But if we put a motion sensor on that light, the rules become a lot more complicated:

- Check for motion every three seconds.
- If anything is moving, is it human sized? (You don't want the light to go on because a cat ran by.)
- If so, turn on the light.
- Check for motion every three seconds.
- Is anything moving?
- If no, wait for 10 seconds, then turn off the lights.

Of course, all of these rules are debatable. Is three seconds too long to check? Or too much: will it use too much power checking that often? Maybe you want the light to turn on when a cat runs by. And I think many of us have a story about being in a bathroom stall and having the lights go out because the sensor didn't detect any motion—maybe 10 seconds is too brief. Needless to say, the rules affect user experience by determining what happens and in what order.

---

2. Of course, this isn't exactly physically how a light switch works. Flipping the switch completes an electric circuit—a circular path—which allows electrons to flow to the lightbulb. Flipping the switch again breaks the circuit. But users don't need to know this; they only need to understand the rule.

Generating Rules

The easiest way to get started with rules is to simply write down all the general rules you know. These are usually the main actions the microinteraction has to perform, in order. For example for adding an item to a shopping cart, the initial rules might be:

1. On an item page, user clicks Add to Cart button.
2. The item is added to the Shopping Cart.

Very straightforward. But as you continue designing, nuance gets added to the rules. For example:

1. On an item page, check to see if the user has purchased this item before. If so, change the button label from Add to Cart to Add Again to Cart.
2. Does the user already have this item in the cart? If so, change Add to Cart to Add Another to Cart.
3. The user clicks button.
4. The item is added to the Shopping Cart.

And so on. And that's just for a button like the one shown in Figure 3-4. There could be many more rules here.

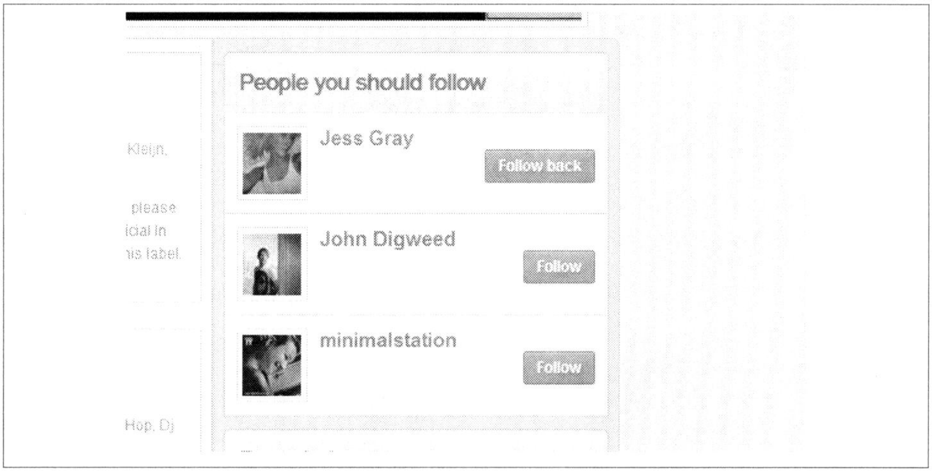

Figure 3-4. A simple button rule. If someone is already following you in Mixcloud, the Follow button becomes Follow back. (Courtesy Murat Mutlu and Little Big Details.)

Of course, rules can also benefit from being visualized. Sometimes a logic diagram can be useful (see Figure 3-5).

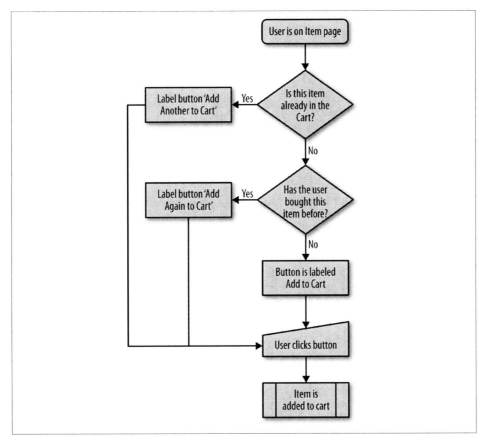

Figure 3-5. An example of a rules logic diagram.

A rules diagram can help you see the rules in a visual way, which can allow you to notice where actions get (overly) complex. It can also show errors in logic that might be hidden by text alone. You can see the effect of nuanced rules in Figure 3-6.

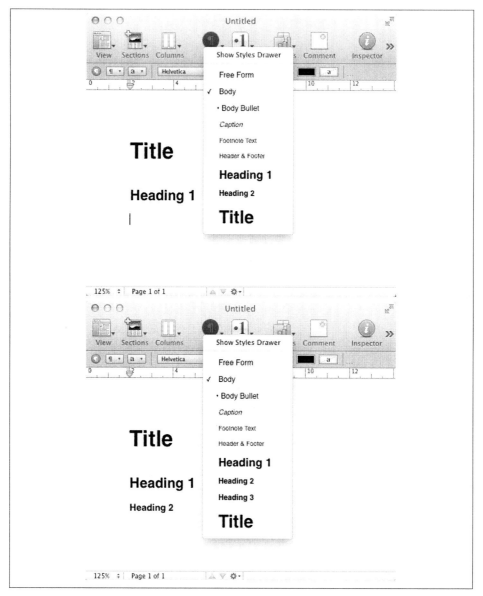

Figure 3-6. Apple's Pages will automatically add smaller heading styles, but only after you've used the smallest displayed style. Heading 3 will only appear as an option once you've used Heading 2. (Courtesy Little Big Details.)

Verbs and Nouns

It can be helpful to think of your entire microinteraction as a sentence. The verbs are the actions that a user can engage in, while the nouns are the objects that enable those actions (Figure 3-7). For example, a slider enables the raising or lowering of volume. Verbs are what the users can do (raise or lower the volume), and nouns are what they do them with (the slider).

Figure 3-7. When friends Like your run on Facebook, you hear cheers in your headphones while using the Nike+ app. (Courtesy Little Big Details.)

Every object in your microinteraction—every piece of UI chrome, every form element, every control, every LED—is a noun with characteristics and states. The rules define what those characteristics and states are (Figure 3-8). Take a simple drop-down menu. It generally has two states: open and closed. When open, it reveals its options, which are some of its characteristics. It could have other characteristics, such as the maximum number of options and the maximum length of any option label. It could also have other states, such as opened with hovers, wherein tool tips appear when a user hovers over options. All of these details should be defined by the rules. (Verbs, too, have characteristics; for example, how fast something is accomplished and how long an action takes. These too should be defined in rules.)

Every noun in your microinteraction should be unique. If you have two of the same nouns, consider combining them. Also make sure that any two (or more) nouns that look the same also behave the same (Figure 3-9). Don't have two similar buttons that act completely different. Objects that behave differently should look differently. Likewise, don't have the same noun work differently in different places. The Back button in Android is famous for being seemingly arbitrary about where it takes the user back to:

sometimes previous modes, sometimes entirely different applications [see Ron Amadeo's article, "Stock Android Isn't Perfect" (*http://bit.ly/17LuYQp*)].

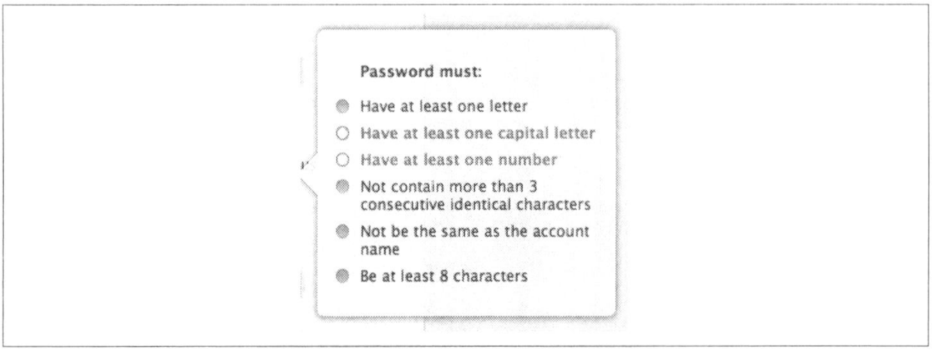

Figure 3-8. When changing your Apple ID password, must-have items are checked off as the user enters them. It reveals the constraints of the microinteraction in a very literal way. (Courtesy Stephen Lewis and Little Big Details.)

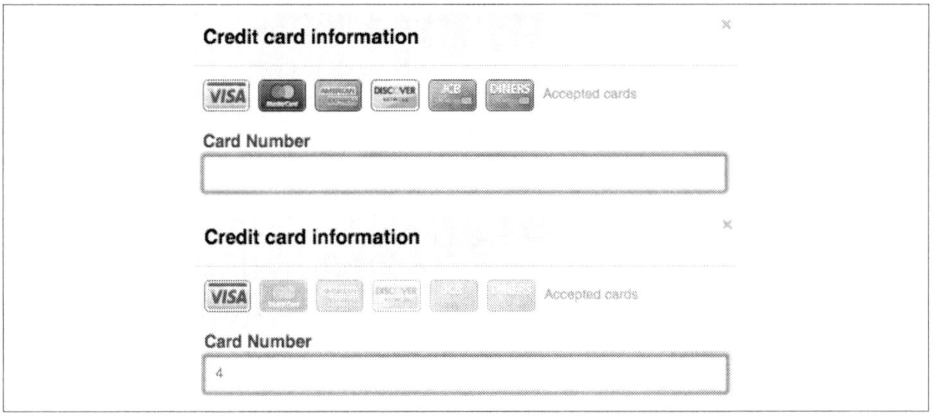

Figure 3-9. GitHub doesn't make users select a credit card. Instead it automatically selects it for them by using the number they type into the field to detect what card type it is. (Courtesy of Little Big Details.)

The best, most elegant microinteractions are often those that allow users a variety of verbs with the fewest possible nouns.

Screens and States

It might be tempting to turn each step of the rules into its own screen; that is, to turn every microinteraction into a wizard-like UI. This works for specific kinds of microinteractions—namely those with defined, discrete steps that are not done often, or are done only once. But for most microinteractions, this would be disruptive and unnecessarily break up the flow of the activity. It's much better to make use of state changes instead. In this way, we use progressive disclosure to reveal only what is necessary at that moment to make a decision or manipulate a control without loading an entirely new screen (see Figure 3-10 for an example).

Figure 3-10. When it comes time to enter the CVV number on the Square iOS app, the image of the credit card flips over so that you can immediately see where the number would be. (Courtesy Dion Almaer.)

As the user steps through the rules, the objects (nouns) inside the microinteraction can (and likely will) change to reflect those changes in time. Each of these is a state that should be designed (Figure 3-11).

Figure 3-11. If multiple friends have their birthdays on the same day, Facebook's birthday microinteraction lets you write on both of their walls at the same time. (Courtesy Marina Janeiko and Little Big Details.)

Any objects the user can interact with can have (at least) three states:

An invitation/default state

This is when the user first finds the object. This is also where prepopulated data can be deployed.

Activated state

What is the object doing while the user is interacting with it?

Updated state

What happens when the user stops interacting with the object?

Let's take a simple drag-and-drop as an example. An object's initial/default state should look draggable. Or, barring that, the object (and/or the cursor) should have a hover state that indicates the object can be dragged. Then the object should likely have another state while being dragged. (It's also possible the screen itself [another noun] at this point has a different state, indicating where the object could be dropped.) And finally, a state when it is at last dropped, which might be simply to return to the default state (Figure 3-12).

Share a link with your followers

SIRENS by @CAMPSTAG: http://youtu.be/fEVEtdGXUl4

Username or email

99 Sign in and Tweet

Password

Remember me · Forgot password?

Figure 3-12. On Twitter, the button to share a link has two idle states: signed in and not signed in. If not signed in, the button allows users to do both at once. (Courtesy Rich Dooley and Little Big Details.)

A designer of microinteractions pays attention to each state, namely because each state can convey information to the user about what is happening—even if what is happening is nothing.

Constraints

The rules have to take into account business, environmental, and technical constraints (Figure 3-13). These can include, but certainly aren't limited to:

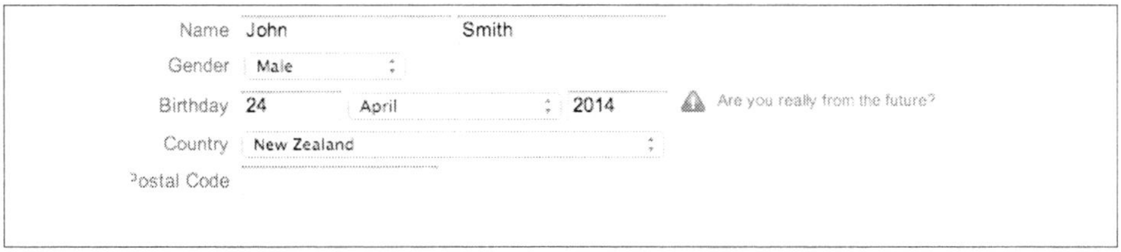

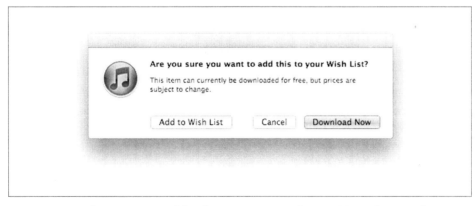

Name
John
Smith
Gender
Male
Birthday
24
April
2014
Are you really from the future?
Country
New Zealand
Postal Code

Figure 3-13. Yahoo! has a sign up microinteraction that won't let you put in a future date. Making that field a drop-down with only acceptable years would prevent this error entirely. (Courtesy Little Big Details.)

- *What input and output methods are available.* Is there a keyboard? A speaker?
- *What is the type or range of any input.* For example, the number of characters allowed in a password, or the maximum volume a user can turn the sound up to.
- *What is expensive.* Not just what costs money (such as access to certain data services, as in Figure 3-14), but also what is expensive from a resources standpoint. Perhaps doing a call to the server every 10 seconds would be a massive hit to the server load and drain the device battery too quickly.
- *What kind of data is available.* What can be collected from sensors? What services/APIs can we access to get information about location, news, weather, time, etc.
- *What kind of data can be collected.* What personal (behavioral) data can be collected and used?

Are you sure you want to add this to your Wish List?
This item can currently be downloaded for free, but prices are subject to change.
Add to Wish List
Cancel
Download Now

Figure 3-14. When trying to add a free item to a Wish List, iTunes lets you know you can just download it for free instead. (Courtesy Little Big Details.)

These last two constraints allow you to not start from zero.

Don't Start from Zero

After the trigger has been initiated, the first question for any microinteraction should be: what do I know about the user and the context? You almost always know something, and that something can be used to improve the microinteraction (Figure 3-15).

Figure 3-15. The Eventbrite iOS app increases the brightness of the Mobile Ticket screen for easier scanning of the QR code. Useful for the context. The alert is probably unnecessary, however. (Courtesy Phil Metcalfe and Little Big Details.)

Some examples of data that could be used:

- What platform/device is being used
- The time of day
- The noise in the room
- How long since the microinteraction was last used
- Is the user in a meeting

- Is the user alone
- The battery life
- The location and/or direction
- What the user has done in the past

Data can even be useful when it doesn't come directly from the user (Figure 3-16).

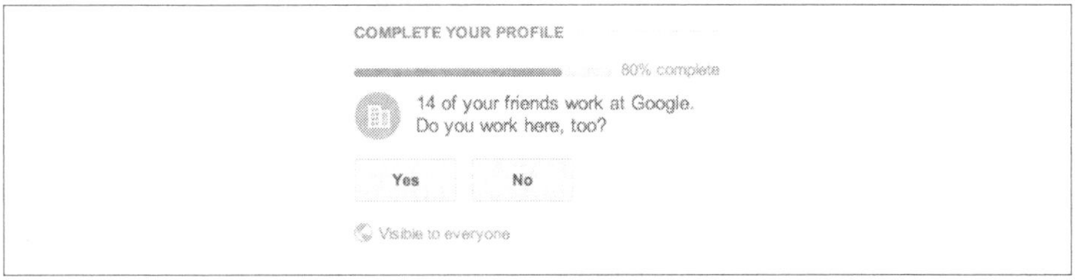

Figure 3-16. Google+ guesses where you work based on your friends' employment. (Courtesy Artem Gassan and Little Big Details.)

That last piece of data—which may be the most important one—relies on collecting information about user behavior, but we're long since past the point where this should be an issue from a system resources point of view; even low-powered appliances have enough memory and processing power to do it. It's just whether or not human resources (developers) can be convinced it's worthwhile. (It is.) Of course, designers should be cognizant of privacy; if the microinteraction deals with sensitive subject matter such as medical information, you might reconsider collecting personal behavior. Ask: could the information that the microinteraction collects be used to embarrass, shame, or endanger users? If so, don't collect it. It's better to have a depersonalized experience than one that is fraught with fear of exposure (Figure 3-17).

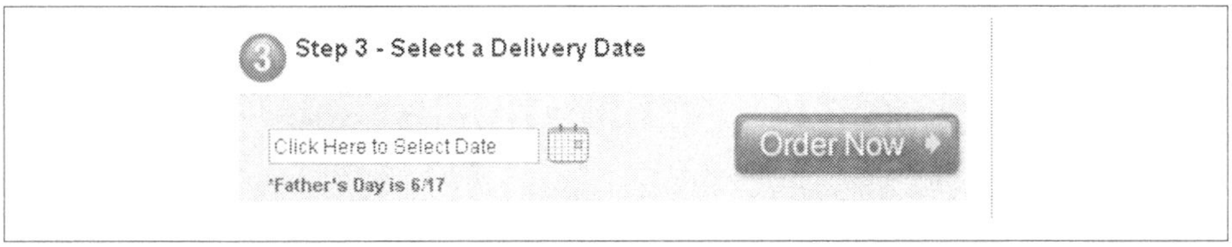

Figure 3-17. Pro Flowers uses the date to show you the next big holiday when selecting a delivery date. (Courtesy Gabriel Henrique and Little Big Details.)

Many of these pieces of data can be used in combination: at 10:00 every day, the user does X, so perhaps when the microinteraction is triggered at that time, offer her X. Or every time the user is in a particular location that he hasn't been to in a while, he does

X. Or every time the user logs in from her mobile device, she's interested in seeing Y. You can see an example of this in Figure 3-18.

Figure 3-18. Threadless lets you know when you first land on the site whether it can ship to the country you're in or not. (Courtesy Little Big Details.)

The point is to use the context and previous behavior (if any) to predict or enhance the microinteraction (Figure 3-19). This data collection can be thought of as ongoing user research; with some analysis you can see how people are using the microinteraction and adjust accordingly. For example, by collecting behavioral data, you might discover that power users could employ an invisible trigger to get them to a certain point in the rules. Navigation app Waze lets power users slide (instead of push) a button to get directly to Navigation, saving two taps.

Safari

Downloads
Dropbox.dmg
25.9 MB
Clear   1 Download

1. Run the Dropbox Installer

From your browser's Downloads window, double click the .dmg file that just downloaded.

Chrome

Dropbox.dmg

1. Run the Dropbox Installer

Click on the .dmg file that just downloaded in the lower left corner of your browser window.

Figure 3-19. Dropbox changes the download instructions based on which browser you're using. (Courtesy Mikko Leino and Little Big Details.)

Absorb Complexity

Larry Tesler, the inventor of cut and paste whom we met back in Chapter 1, came up with an axiom that is important to keep in mind when designing rules: Tesler's Law of the Conservation of Complexity. Tesler's Law, briefly stated, says that all activities have an inherent complexity; there is a point beyond which you cannot simplify a process any further. The only question then becomes what to do with that complexity. Either the system handles it and thus removes control from the user, or else the user handles it, pushing more decisions—yet more control—onto the user (Figure 3-20).

Figure 3-20. Even in the clunky iCal, there is a nice rule in the selection of a time microinteraction. Rather than have you do the math to figure out how long an event would be, iCal shows you event duration when selecting the end time. It's an effective use of microcopy. (Courtesy Jack Moffett.)

For microinteractions, you're going to want to err on the side of removing control and having the microinteraction handle most of the decision making. One caveat to this is that some microinteractions are completely about giving control to the user, but even then there is likely to be complexity that the system should handle (Figure 3-21).

Start by figuring out where the core complexity lies, then decide which parts of that the user might like to have, and when in the overall process. Then, if control is absolutely necessary, provide it at that time (Figure 3-22).

Computers are simply much better at handling some kinds of complexity than humans. If any of these are in your microinteraction, have the system handle it:

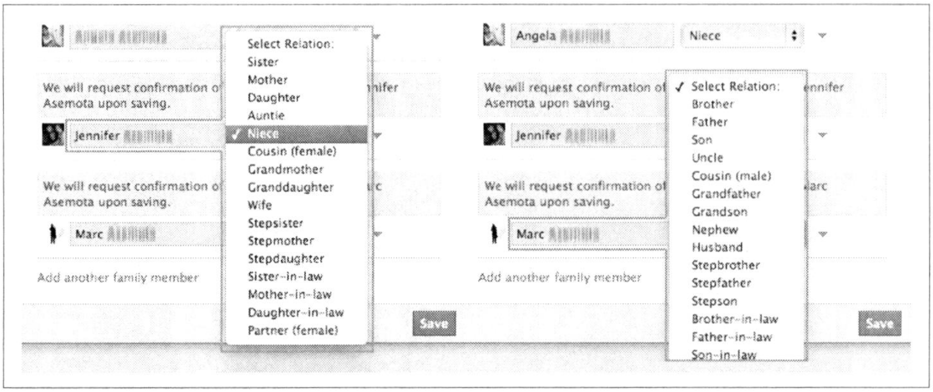

Figure 3-21. When you add a new family member on Facebook, Facebook automatically recognizes the chosen family member's gender and adjusts the list of possible familial relationships in the list box accordingly. (Courtesy Stefan Asemota and Little Big Details.)

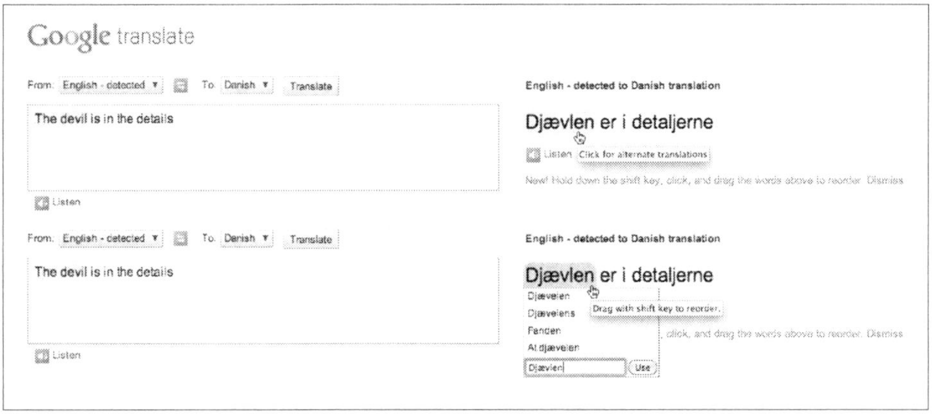

Figure 3-22. When hovering over the translation in Google Translate, it highlights the translated phrase in the original text. You can get alternate translations, but only by clicking on the original text. (Courtesy Shruti Ramiah and Little Big Details.)

- Rapidly performing computation and calculations
- Doing multiple tasks simultaneously
- Unfailingly remembering things
- Detecting complicated patterns
- Searching through large datasets for particular item(s)

Of course, removing complexity means you must be smart about the choices you do offer and the defaults you have.

Limited Options and Smart Defaults

The more options that you give a user, the more rules a microinteraction has to have, and in general, fewer rules make for better, more understandable microinteractions. This means limiting the choices you give to the user and instead presenting smart defaults.

With microinteractions, a good practice is to emphasize (or perform automatically) the next action the user is most likely to take. This emphasis can be can be done by removing any other options, or just by visual means (making the button large, for instance). As game designer Jesse Schell put it in his book *The Art of Game Design* (CRC Press), "If you can control where someone is going to look, you can control where they are going to go."

Knowing the next likely step is also valuable in that you can perform or present that step automatically, without the user having to do anything else (see Figures 3-23 and 3-24). This is one way to link microinteractions together (see the section "Orchestrating Microinteractions" on page 137 in Chapter 6).

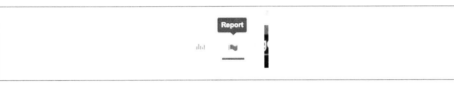

Figure 3-23. Clicking the Report button on YouTube automatically stops the video you're about to report. It performs the next likely action for you. (Courtesy Aaron Laibson and Little Big Details.)

Every option a user has is at least another rule, so *the best way to keep your rules to a minimum is to limit options*. In short, be ruthless in eliminating options. Microinteractions do one thing well, so ideally the user would have no options, just smart defaults throughout the entire microinteraction. Everyone does one action, and that action plays out: from Rule 1 to Rule 2 to Rule 3. This is what made Google's search box the most effective (or at least the most used online) microinteraction of the early 21st century. Everyone followed the same rules:

- Enter text and press (the emphasized) search button.
- Show search results.

Figure 3-24. Any selected text on a page will prepopulate the caption field when adding it to Pinterest. (Courtesy Louisa Fosco and Little Big Details.)

Of course, even here Google added an option: the I'm Feeling Lucky button, which took you directly to the top search result. I'm Feeling Lucky was only used by 1% of users…and reportedly cost Google $100 million a year in lost ad revenues. In 2010, Google effectively killed I'm Feeling Lucky when it introduced Google Instant, which immediately started showing search results as you type, so there is no chance to press the I'm Feeling Lucky button.[3] Now the rules look like this:

- Enter text.
- Show search results.

It literally cannot get any simpler, unless at some point in the future Google is able to guess what you want to search on and immediately shows you results.

For microinteractions, more than one major option is probably too many. This is not to say you cannot have choices, such as a temperature setting (hot, warm, cold), but rather more than one option that radically changes the rules is ill advised. It's likely that this kind of change puts the microinteraction into a different mode (see Chapter 5). One common example of this is the Forgot Your Password? Mode that many login microinteractions have. Clicking that link takes the user into a different mode that hopefully, eventually takes the user back to the main mode to enter the remembered password.

If you are going to make a default decision for a user, in some instances there should be some indication of what that decision is. One example is Apple's Calendar notifications. When a calendar notification appears (e.g., "Meeting in 15 minutes") there is a Snooze button the user can press. However, there is no indication of the duration of that snooze (as it turns out, it's, in my opinion, an overly long 15-minute snooze) and there's no way

---

3. Nicholas Carlson, "Google Just Killed The 'I'm Feeling Lucky Button,'" *Business Insider*, September 8, 2010.

to change this default. "Snooze 15 Minutes" would be a better button label: one that indicates what the rule is.

The most prominent default should be the action that most people do most of the time. Even if you decide that this shouldn't be automatically done for the user, it should be visually prominent. The most common example of this are OK/Cancel buttons. Cancel is likely pressed considerably less often than OK, so OK should be more easily seen (larger and/or colored). And don't forget the Return key (if there is one). Pressing Return should perform the default action.

If you have to present a choice to the user, remember that how you present that choice can affect what is chosen. Items at the top and bottom of a list are better recalled than those in the middle. A highlighted option is more often selected than one that is not. And if the user has to make a series of decisions, start with simpler, broader decisions, and move toward more detailed options. Colleen Roller, Vice President of Usability for Bank of America Merrill Lynch, rightly says that, "People feel most confident in their decisions when they understand the available options and can comfortably compare and evaluate each one. It's easiest to evaluate the options when there are only a few of them, and they are easily distinguishable from each other."[4]

Since every option means (at least) one other rule (and remember we're trying to keep rules to as few as possible), the options you present to a user have to be *meaningful.* Meaningful choices affect how the user achieves the goal of the microinteraction—or even what the goal is. An example of a meaningful choice might be to sign in via Facebook or to enter a username/password. Nonmeaningful choices are those that don't affect the outcome no matter what is chosen. Amazon's Kindle app makes users select what color highlight they want to highlight passages in, even though you can't search or export by highlight color; it's only marginally meaningful and should probably have been left out of the default microinteraction of highlighting. Ask: is giving this choice to a user going to make the experience more interesting, valuable, or pleasurable? If the answer is no, leave it out.

The elimination of choice should have one beneficial side effect: the removal of many possible edge cases. Edges cases are those challenging-to-resolve problems that occur only occasionally, typically for a small minority of (power) users. Edge cases can cause your microinteraction to warp so that you are designing to accommodate unusual use cases, not the most common. Edge cases are kryptonite for microinteractions, and everything possible should be done to avoid them, including revising rules to make them impossible. For example, if a Year of Birth form field is a text box, it's easy to put in invalid dates, such as those in the future. Remove this edge case by making the field a drop-down menu.

---

4. "Abundance of Choice and Its Effect on Decision Making," *UX Matters*, December 6, 2010.

Controls and User Input

Most microinteractions have some place for manual user input. What has to be decided is which controls, and how they manifest. Take something as simple as a volume microinteraction. Volume can have three states: louder, quieter, and muted. These could appear as three buttons, a slider, a dial, two buttons, a scroll wheel, a slider and a button, and probably several other variations as well.

With controls, the choice is between operational simplicity and perceived simplicity (Figure 3-25). Operational simplicity gives every command its own control. In our volume example, this is the three-button solution: one button for Make Louder, one button to Make Quieter, one button for Mute. With perceived simplicity, a single control does multiple actions. For volume, this would mean selecting the slider or scroll-wheel options.

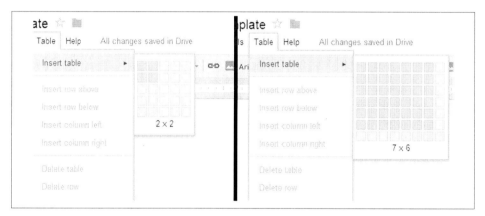

Figure 3-25. Google Drive's Insert Table microinteraction has an expanding hover window that lets users visually determine the size of the table. (Courtesy Kjetil Holmefjord and Little Big Details.)

For microinteractions that will be done repeatedly, err on the side of perceived simplicity, unless it is an action that needs to be done quickly and with no chance of error—for example, the Mute button on a conference phone; combining it with the Make Quieter action would probably be a disaster. For microinteractions that will only be done once or occasionally, err on the side of operational simplicity; display all the options so that little to no foreknowledge is required.

Text fields should be forgiving of what is placed in them and assume that the text could be coming from any number of places, particularly from the clipboard or the user's memory. For example, a form for a telephone number should support users putting in any of the following: (415) 555-1212, 4155551212, or 415-555-1212. Text fields in particular need what system designers call requisite variety—the ability to survive under varied conditions. Often this means "fixing" input behind the scenes in code so that all the varied inputs conform to the format that the code/database needs (see Figure 3-26 for a poor example and Figure 3-27 for a positive one).

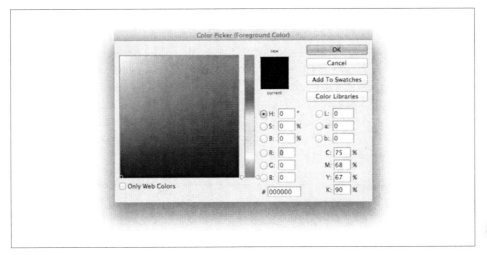

Figure 3-26. Adobe Photoshop's Color Picker microinteraction has a place to enter a hex value. However, it's not smart enough to strip out the # if one is pasted into it. (Courtesy Jack Moffett.)

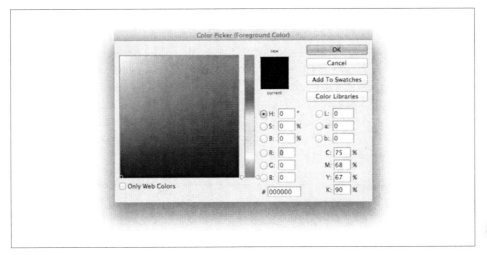

Figure 3-27. 37signals' Basecamp gets it right. When you paste an email ID like "Jane Smith <myemail@gmail.com>," it automatically strips out everything extraneous and leaves just the email address. (Courtesy Harpal Singe and Little Big Details.)

Ordering of lists, such as in a drop-down menu, should be carefully thought out. Sometimes it makes sense to have a predetermined scheme, such as alphabetical or last used. Other times, it might make more sense to be seemingly illogical. For example, if most of your users come from the United States, it makes no sense to have them scroll through the previous 20 letters of the alphabet to reach the U countries—be seemingly irrational and put it at the top of the list or else just make it the default.

Sometimes it makes sense to have redundant controls. Particularly if your microinteraction is going to be used frequently by the same user, it may be wise to design in shortcuts. In desktop software, these have traditionally been keyboard shortcuts such as Command-Q for Quit, while on touchscreen devices and trackpads they have been a gesture (usually multitouch). Just make sure that no significant (to the activity flow) control is buried under a shortcut. For any important action, there should be a visible, manual way to engage with it.

Preventing Errors

One of the main tasks for rules should be error prevention (see Figures 3-28 and 3-29). Microinteractions should follow the Poka-Yoke ("mistake proofing") Principle, which was created in the 1960s by Toyota's legendary industrial engineer Shigeo Shingo. Poka-Yoke says that products and processes should be designed so that it's impossible for users to commit an error because the product/process simply won't allow one. One quick example of Poka-Yoke in action is Apple's Lightning cable. Unlike their previous 30-pin connector (and every USB cord), the Lightning cable can be plugged in to the iPhone's or iPad's port in any orientation. Unlike with a USB cable, you can't try to put it in upside down (where it won't fit) because it fits either way.

Figure 3-28. Gmail gives you a notification before sending the mail to see if you've forgotten to attach a file. (Courtesy Little Big Details.)

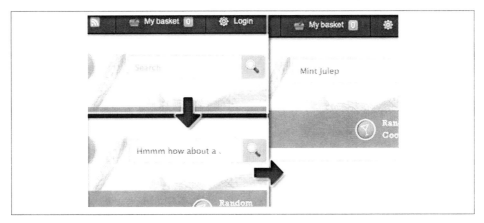

Figure 3-29. If you press the search button on Make Me a Cocktail with nothing in the search field, instead of displaying an error message or nothing, it shows a random cocktail. (Courtesy Nick Wilkins and Little Big Details.)

Similarly, you want to design your microinteraction so that the rules don't allow for mistakes to be made (Figure 3-30). This may mean reducing user control and input, but for microinteractions reducing choice is seldom a bad practice.

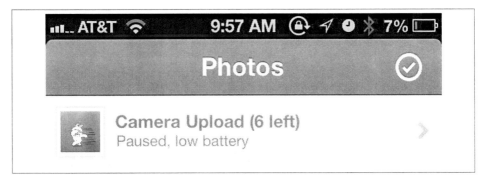

Figure 3-30. Dropbox for iOS pauses uploads when there is a low battery. (Courtesy Little Big Details.)

Ideally, your microinteraction should be designed so that it does not present an error message when the user has done everything right (because the user shouldn't be able to do anything wrong), and only presents an error message when the system itself cannot respond properly. Pop-up error alerts are the tool of the lazy. If an error does occur, the microinteraction should do everything in its power to fix it first (see Figure 3-31).

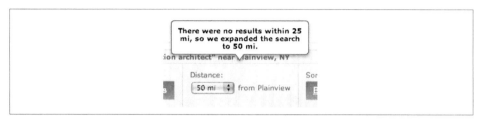

Figure 3-31. Meetup.com adjusts your search results to attempt to correct the error of no found results. (Courtesy Michael J. Morgan and Little Big Details.)

Using the rules, you can also prevent people from using your microinteraction in ways it wasn't intended to be used (see Figures 3-32 and 3-33). For example, you could disallow expletives in comments.

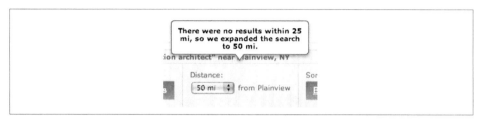

Figure 3-32. What do you love? won't let you enter expletives. It just changes the word to "kittens" and shows those results instead. (Courtesy Zachary Reese.)

Microcopy

Microcopy—labels, instructions, and other tiny pieces of text—is part of understanding the rules. Microcopy is a kind of fixed feedback or feedforward. The entirety of a microinteraction can be a single piece of microcopy: look at Facebook's Like "button," which is based entirely on the word Like in blue text.

A system trigger could cause an essential piece of microcopy to appear when it would be most helpful. For example, on a store's Contact page, a "Sorry, we're closed" message

Figure 3-33. Twitter won't let you tweet the same message twice, mostly to protect its service from abuse. Detecting a duplicate before the user presses Send would be better, although more system-resource intense. (Courtesy Sindre Sorhus and Little Big Details.)

could appear beside the phone number during off hours. And that would be the entire microinteraction right there!

With almost all microinteractions, you want to first make sure any text is absolutely necessary for understanding; instructional copy for microinteractions often isn't. You don't usually have to put "Please log in" at the top of a login form for users to understand that is what they should do. If you do need to include text, make sure it is as short as possible. As Winston Churchill so aptly put it, "The short words are the best, and the old words best of all."

Never use instructional copy when a label will suffice. Tap Next to Continue is unnecessary if there is a button labeled Next or Continue. If a label, such as the name of an album, has to be truncated (for space), there should be a way to see the full title on hover or rollover (desktop/web apps) or tap/click (mobile). Sometimes, particularly with physical buttons, there isn't enough space for a word and manufacturers try to put part of the word on the control, ending up with a letter jumble that resembles a customized license plate. This is not recommended. If a word doesn't fit, consider an icon instead.

Avoid labels that could be misinterpreted. On photo-sharing service Flickr, for instance, the two choices to navigate photos are ← Previous and Next →. However, Previous takes you to the next newer photo, while Next takes you to the next older photo (Figure 3-34).

Figure 3-34. Microsoft's Powerpoint transparency slider in the Ribbon. There is no label to indicate if you're making it more or less transparent, and the change doesn't occur until after you release the slider. (Courtesy Jack Moffett.)

The best place for most labels is above what is going to be manipulated. The second best place is on or in the object to be manipulated, as Luke Wroblewski notes in "Top, Right, or Left-Aligned Form Labels" (*http://bit.ly/ZCfWG0*) and "Web Form Design: Labels Within Inputs" (*http://bit.ly/13mqT1x*) . This is because it only requires a single-eye fixation to take in both the label and the object. In other words, the eye doesn't have to spend time moving between two objects, which the mind then has to connect.[5] However, the tradition with icons is the label goes below the icon.

Be careful putting a label inside a text form field. When it disappears (as it must because the user clicks into it to put text there), the user can forget what the field is for, and there is no easy way of going back short of clicking out of the text field. It's better in some cases to put the label above (Toy Search) or on a button (Search for Toys) alongside, with examples (e.g., "board games, Lego, or dolls") in the text form field itself.

Be sure that any instructional copy matches the control exactly. For example, don't have the instructions read, "Add items to your shopping cart," then have the button say, Purchase Objects instead of Add Items.

When possible, make text relational instead of exact, particularly dates and times. "Three hours ago" is much easier to understand than showing a date and time stamp, which causes users to make translations and calculations in their head as to when that was. (Of course, sometimes an exact date or time is necessary and shouldn't be obscured, as in Figure 3-35.)

Avoid double (or more!) negatives, unless your intention is to confuse or deliberately mislead people. "If you don't want to unsubscribe to our email newsletter, don't uncheck this box."

Algorithms

In 1832, a 17-year-old self-taught son of a shoemaker had a vision of how "a mind most readily accumulates knowledge ... that man's mind works by means of some mechanism." Twenty-two years later, as a university professor, this former child prodigy published his masterpiece: *An Investigation of the Laws of Thought, On Which Are Founded the Mathematical Theories of Logic and Probability.* (Like many masterpieces, it was criticized, dismissed, or simply ignored when it was first published.) That professor's name was George Boole, and he was the father of what we now know of as Boolean logic.

---

5. For more on eye fixations, see J. Edward Russo, "Eye Fixations Can Save the World: A Critical Evaluation" and "A Comparison Between Eye Fixations and Other Information Processing Methodologies," in *Advances in Consumer Research* Volume 05. 561–570 (1978).

Figure 3-35. Budge's setting screen for To Do Reminders uses clear copy and choices to make what could have been a boring form interesting. (Courtesy Paula Te and Little Big Details.)

Boole devised a kind of linguistic algebra, in which the three basic operations are AND, OR, and NOT. These operations form the basis for generating algorithms. Algorithms are, in the words of Christopher Steiner in *Automate This: How Algorithms Came to Rule Our World* (Portfolio Hardcover):

> Giant decision trees composed of one binary decision after another. Almost everything we do, from driving a car to trading a stock to picking a spouse, can be broken down to a string of binary decisions based on binary input.
>
> [...]
>
> At its core, an algorithm is a set of instructions to be carried out perfunctorily to achieve an ideal result. Information goes into a given algorithm, answers come out.

Although the rules could, in a meta fashion, be thought of algorithmically, some microinteractions depend on algorithms to run. For example, take search. What appears in autofill—not to mention the order of the results themselves—is all generated by an algorithm (Figure 3-36). Recommendations, driving directions, and most emailed/read are all generated algorithmically. Some branded elements, such as Nike FuelBand's NikeFuel points, are based on an algorithm, as is the custom color picker in FiftyThree's outstanding iPad app, Paper.[6]

Traditionally, these algorithms have all been generated by engineers, but as more and more products come to rely on algorithms, it behooves designers to get involved in their design. After all, a beautiful search microinteraction is meaningless without valuable search results.

Figure 3-36. If you're watching a music video on YouTube, it algorithmically matches your location to the artist's touring schedule. (Courtesy of Nanakoe and Little Big Details.)

While the code behind algorithms is far too complex to get into here, defining the algorithm is. There are four major parts to any algorithm:

Sequence
> What are the steps in the process? What item comes before what? Are there any conditionals, where an action is dependent on a particular condition? For a device like the Nike FuelBand, this might be something like: for every two steps (as measured by an accelerometer in the hardware), add one to NikeFuel.

Decisions
> These are usually in the form of if ... then statements. For example, if the time is 00:00, then reset.

Repetitions
> How does the algorithm loop? This can be the whole algorithm, or just a particular sequence. For example, while the user is typing in the search field, update search results every time there is a new letter.

---

6. See "The Magical Tech Behind Paper For iPad's Color-Mixing Perfection," by Chris Dannen in *Fast Company*, November 8, 2012.

Variables

Variables are containers for the data that powers algorithms. Defining these will allow you to tweak the algorithm without having to rewrite it entirely. Number of Search Results could be a variable, as could Number of Steps Taken. Variables are numeric, alphabetic (text), or logical (true/false).

To put this all together, let's say a microinteraction involves displaying music recommendations. The steps in the sequence are the kinds of music you want to show, and in what order. Are they all from one genre? Does new music take priority over old? Decisions might include: has the user ever listened to this artist before? If so, do not recommend. The algorithm might loop until all the recommendations are filled. And variables could be genre, artist, album, listened to, similar to, tempo, and a whole host of possible characteristics one could use to match music. Variables could also include values such as the percentage of new music to old, and the total number of recommendations to show.

It can be helpful for users to know what data/variables are being acted upon in an algorithm, so that they can manually adjust them if possible. For example, knowing how your FuelBand adds FuelPoints would be valuable so that users could increase their activity appropriately. As it is now, it's a bit of a mystery. Of course, some algorithms, such as Google's search algorithm, are deeply complex and could not be easily explained, especially in microcopy.

What is important to keep in mind from a microinteraction design standpoint is what the user is intending to do, and what data/content is going to be the most valuable, then ensure that those human values get baked into the algorithm. Too often, and too easily, algorithms can be designed solely for efficiency, not for value.

The trouble with rules is that, in the end, they are invisible. Users can only figure them out when something drastic happens, like Apple's change to Save As, or from the feedback the system provides, which is the subject of Chapter 4.

Summary

Rules create a nontechnical model of the microinteraction. They define what can and cannot be done, and in what order.

Rules must reflect constraints. Business, contextual, and technical constraints must be handled.

Don't start from zero. Use what you know about the user, the platform, or the environment to improve the microinteraction.

Remove complexity. Reduce controls to a minimum.

Reduce options and make smart defaults. More options means more rules.

Define states for each object. How do the items change over time or with interactivity?

Err on the side of perceived simplicity. Do more with less.

Use the rules to prevent errors. Make human errors impossible.

Keep copy short. Never use instructional text where a label will suffice.

Help define algorithms. Keep human values in coded decision making.

CHAPTER 4

Feedback

A 56-year-old man punched his fist through the glass and into the electronics of the machine. "Yes, I broke the machine and I'd do it again," he told the security guards. (He was sentenced to 90 days in jail.) Another man, 59-year-old Douglas Batiste, was also arrested for assaulting a machine—by urinating on it. A woman caused $1,800 in damages to another machine by slapping it three times.[1] And 67-year-old Albert Lee Clark, after complaining to an employee and getting no satisfaction, went to his car and got his gun. He came back inside and shot the machine several times.[2]

What device is causing so much rage? Slot machines.

Slot machines are a multi-billion-dollar business. Slot machines take in $7 out of every $10 spent on gambling. Collectively, the money they generate is in the tens of billions,

---

1. Nir, Sarah Maslin, "Failing to Hit Jackpot, and Hitting Machine Instead," The *New York Times*, July 13, 2012.

2. "Man charged with shooting slot machine," Associated Press, February 13, 2012.

far surpassing the revenue of other forms of entertainment, such as movies, video games, and even pornography.[3] The reason that slot machines—microinteraction devices for sure—work so well at taking money from people is because of the feedback they provide. Most (read: all) of this feedback is insidious, designed specifically to keep people playing for as long as possible.

If you are the statistical anomaly who has never seen or played a slot machine, they work like this: you put coins, bills, or (in newer machines) paper tickets with barcodes into the machine. Pushing a button, tapping the touchscreen, or pulling a lever (the trigger) causes three (or more) seemingly independent "tumblers" to spin. When they stop spinning after a few seconds, if they are aligned in particular ways (if the symbols are the same on all three tumblers, for example), the player is a winner and money drops out of the slot machine. A committed player can do a few hundred (!) spins in an hour.

What really happens is that the rules are rigged in the slot machine's favor; statistically, the slot machine will never pay out more than 90%, so the tumblers never "randomly" do anything, although the feedback makes it seem that way. If the tumblers actually worked the way they appear to work, the payback percentage would be 185% to 297% —obviously an undesirable outcome for casino owners. The outcome is "random but weighted." Blank spaces and low-paying symbols appear more frequently than jackpot symbols—that is, less frequently than they would if the tumbler were actually (instead of just seemingly) random. Thanks to the feedback they get, players have no idea what the actual weighting is; an identical model can be weighted differently than the machine next to it. Since modern slot machines are networked devices, the weighting can even be adjusted from afar, on the fly.[4]

No matter how players trigger the tumblers—by pulling the lever harder, for example —players cannot influence or change the outcome. Some slot machines also have a stop button to stop the tumbler "manually" while they spin. This too doesn't affect the outcome; it only provides an illusion of control.[5]

Not only are the tumblers weighted to prevent winning, but they are designed to incite what gambling researcher Kevin Harrigan calls the Aww Shucks Effect by frequently halting on a "near win," or a failure that's close to a success (see Figure 4-1). For example, the first two tumblers show the same symbol, but the third is blank. These near wins occur 12 times more often than they would by chance alone. Research has shown that

---

3. Rivlin, Gary, "The Tug of the Newfangled Slot Machines," The *New York Times*, May 9, 2004.

4. Richtel, Matt, "From the Back Office, a Casino Can Change the Slot Machine in Seconds," The *New York Times*, April 12, 2006.

5. All from Kevin Harrigan's "The Design of Slot Machine Games," 2009.

---

near wins make people want to gamble more by activating the parts of the brain that are associated by wins—even though they didn't win![6]

Figure 4-1. An example of a "near win." (Courtesy Marco Verch.)

When a player does win, the win is usually small, although the feedback is disproportionate to the winning, so that players think they've won big. Lights flash, sounds play. And the sounds! In the *New York Times* profile of slot machine designer Joe Kaminkow, it notes:

> Before Kaminkow's arrival, [slot machine manufacturer] I.G.T.'s games weren't quiet— hardly—but they didn't take full advantage of the power of special effects like "smart sounds"—bright bursts of music. So Kaminkow decreed that every action, every spin of the wheel, every outcome, would have its own unique sound. The typical slot machine featured maybe 15 "sound events" when Kaminkow first arrived at I.G.T. [in 1999]; now that average is closer to 400. And the deeper a player gets into a game, the quicker and usually louder the music.[7]

---

6. Clark, L, Laurence, A., Astley-Jones, F., Gray, N., "Gambling near-misses enhance motivation to gamble and recruit brain-related circuitry," *Neuron* 61, 2009.

7. Rivlin, Gary, "The Tug of the Newfangled Slot Machines." The *New York Times*.

The slot machine microinteraction is so addictive because it provides, via feedback, *intermittent reinforcement of behavior*. Slot machine players keep performing the same behavior until they are eventually rewarded. With slot machines, if payout was predictable—if the player won every other time, for example—players would quickly get bored or annoyed. What keeps people playing is the very unpredictability of the payouts, plus the promise that very rarely there will be a big jackpot. In general, this is *not* the kind of reinforcement you want for most microinteractions, where you want consistent feedback with positive reinforcement (via feedback) of desirable behavior. Predictability is desirable.

Slot machines teach us that feedback is extremely powerful and can make or break a microinteraction. Visuals and sound combine to make an engaging experience out of what could be a repetitive, dull activity of pulling a lever over and over. Obviously, they do this to their mind-blowingly lucrative benefit and you certainly don't want every microinteraction being like a flashing, noisy slot machine, but the lesson is the same: feedback provides the character, the personality, of the microinteraction.

Feedback Illuminates the Rules

Unlike slot machines, which are designed to deliberately obscure the rules, with microinteractions the true purpose of feedback is to help users understand how the rules of the microinteraction work. If a user pushes a button, something should happen that indicates two things: that the button has been pushed, and what has happened as a result of that button being pushed (Figure 4-2). Slot machines will certainly tell you the first half (that the lever was pulled), just not the second half (what is happening behind the scenes) because if they did, people probably wouldn't play—or at least not as much. But since feedback doesn't have to tell users how the microinteraction *actually* works—what the rules actually are—the feedback should be just enough for users to make a working mental model of the microinteraction. Along with the affordances of the trigger, feedback should let users know what they can and cannot do with the microinteraction.

One caveat: you can have legitimate, nondeceitful reasons for not wanting users to know how the rules work; for example, users may not need to know every time a sensor is triggered or every time the device goes out to fetch data, only if something significant changes. For example, you don't often need to know when there is no new email message, only when there is a new one. *The first principle of feedback for microinteractions is to not overburden users with feedback*. Ask: what is the least amount of feedback that can be delivered to convey what is going on (Figure 4-3)?

Off
Create a Batch
Select a Batch
Done
On
Create a Batch
Select a Batch
Done

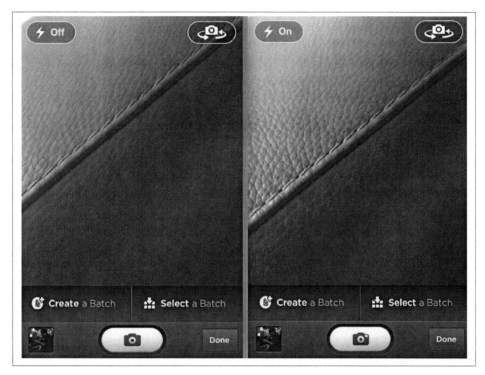

Figure 4-2. In Batch, when the flash is on, the camera icon on the shutter button gets a white flash indicator. (Courtesy Little Big Details.)

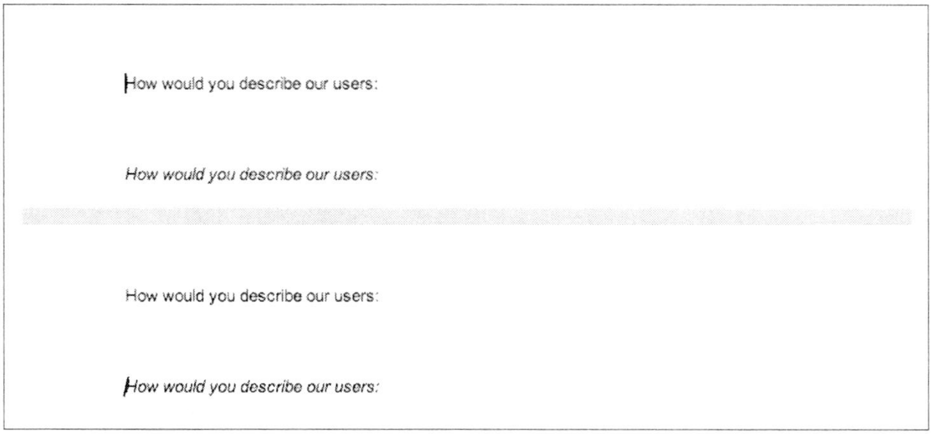

How would you describe our users:
How would you describe our users:
How would you describe our users:
How would you describe our users:

Figure 4-3. Google Docs slants the cursor when you're typing in italics. Microsoft Word does this as well. (Courtesy Gregg Bernstein and Little Big Details.)

Feedback should be driven by need: what does the user need to know and when (how often)? Then it is up to the designer to determine what format that feedback should take: visual, audible, or haptic, or some combination thereof (see Figures 4-4 and 4-5).

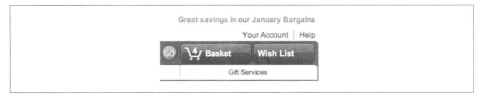

Figure 4-4. Amazon puts the item counter inside the shopping cart button. (Courtesy Matthew Solle and Little Big Details.)

Figure 4-5. Sometimes it's important to indicate what didn't happen. When recommending an app via email, Apple's App Store tells you that you haven't been added to any email lists. (Courtesy Little Big Details.)

Feedback should occur:

- *Immediately after a manual trigger or following/during a manual adjustment of a rule.* All user-initiated actions should be accompanied by a system acknowledgment (see Figure 4-6). Pushing a button should indicate what happened.

- *On any system-initiated triggers in which the state of the microinteraction (or the surrounding feature) has changed significantly.* The significance will vary by context and will have to be determined on a case-by-case basis by the designer. Some microinteractions will (and should) run in the background. An example is an email client checking to see if there are new messages. Users might not need to know every time it checks, but will want to know when there are new messages.

- *Whenever a user reaches the edge (or beyond) of a rule.* This would be the case of an error about to occur. Ideally, this state would never occur, but it's sometimes necessary, such as when a user enters a wrong value (e.g., a password) into a field. Another example is reaching the bottom of a scrolling list when there are no more items to display.

- *Whenever the system cannot execute a command.* For instance, if the microinteraction cannot send a message because the device is offline. One caveat to this is that multiple attempts to execute the command could occur before the feedback that something is amiss. It might take several tries to connect to a network, for example, and knowing this, you might wait to show an error message until after several attempts have been made.

- *Showing progress on any critical process, particularly if that process will take a long time.* If your microinteraction is about uploading or downloading, for example, it would be appropriate to estimate duration of the process (see Figure 4-7).

Figure 4-6. Pixelmator's eyedropper tool shows you the color you've chosen inside the pipette. (Courtesy Little Big Details.)

Feedback could occur:

- *At the beginning or end of a process.* For example, after an item has finished downloading.
- *At the beginning or end of a mode or when switching between modes* (Figure 4-8).

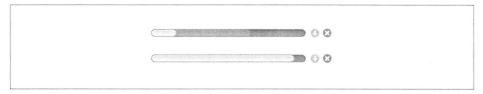

Figure 4-7. Transmit 4 shows in one progress bar both the total transfer and individual transfers. (Courtesy Stef van der Feen and Little Big Details.)

Figure 4-8. On Quora, you can see if someone is answering the question you're looking at. (Courtesy Allison Ko and Little Big Details.)

Always look for moments where the feedback can demystify what the microinteraction is doing; without feedback, the user will never understand the rules.

Feedback Is for Humans

While there is certainly machine-to-machine feedback, the feedback we're most concerned with is communicating to the human beings using the product. For microinteractions, that message is usually one of the following:

- Something has happened
- You did something
- A process has started
- A process has ended
- A process is ongoing
- You can't do that

Once you know what message you want to send, the only decisions remaining are how these messages manifest, as in Figures 4-9 through 4-11. The kind of feedback you can provide depends entirely upon the type of hardware the microinteraction is on. On a mobile phone, you might have visual, audible, and haptic feedback possible. On a piece of consumer electronics, feedback could only be visual, in the form of LEDs.

Figure 4-9. Humans respond to faces. The Boxee logo turns orange and "goes to sleep" when there is no Internet connection. (Courtesy Emil Tullstedt and Little Big Details.)

Figure 4-10. The Threadless shopping cart face turns from frowning to happy when you put items in it. (Courtesy Ahmed Alley and Little Big Details.)

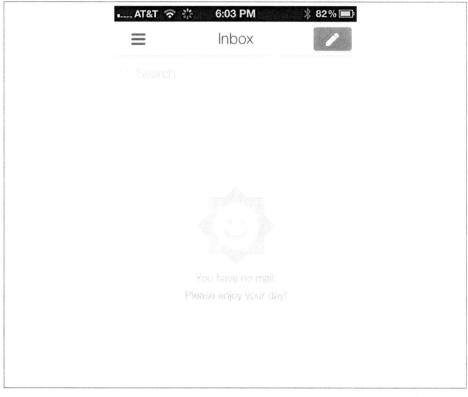

Figure 4-11. The Gmail iPhone app shows what not to do: randomly put a smiley face for a message that isn't necessarily a happy one. (Courtesy Steve Portigal.)

Let's take a microinteraction appliance like a dishwasher as an example. The dishwasher process goes something like this: a user selects a setting, turns the dishwasher on, the dishwasher washes the dishes and stops. If someone opens the dishwasher midprocess, it complains. Now, if the dishwasher has a screen, each of these actions could be accompanied by a message on the screen ("Washing Dishes. 20 minutes until complete."). If there is no screen, there might be only LEDs and sounds to convey these messages. One option might be that an LED blinks while the dishwasher is running, and a chime sounds when the washing cycle is completed.

Text (written) feedback is not always an option (for example, if there is no screen or simply no screen real estate). Once we move past actual words—and let's not forget that a substantial portion of the planet's population is illiterate: 793 million adults, according to the Central Intelligence Agency (*http://1.usa.gov/117Thmr*)—we have to convey messages via other means: sound, iconography, images, light, and haptics. Since they are not text (and even words can be vague and slippery), they can be open to interpretation. What does that blinking LED mean? When the icon changes color, what is it trying to convey? Some feedback is clearly learned over time: when that icon lights up and I click it, I see there is a new message. The "penalty" for clicking (or acting on) any feedback that might be misinterpreted should be none. If I can't guess that the blinking LED means the dishwasher is in use, opening the dishwasher shouldn't spray me with scalding hot water. In fact, neurologically, errors improve performance; how humans learn is when our expectation doesn't match the outcome.

The second principle of feedback is that the best feedback is never arbitrary: it always exists to convey a message that helps users, and there is a deep connection between the action causing the feedback and the feedback itself. Pressing a button to turn on a device and hearing a beep is practically meaningless, as there is no relationship between the trigger (pressing the button) or the resulting action (the device turning on) and the resulting sound. It would be much better to either have a click (the sound of a button being pushed) or some visual/sound cue of the device powering up, such as a note that increases in pitch. Arbitrary feedback makes it harder to connect actions to results, and thus harder for users to understand what is happening. The best microinteractions couple the trigger to the rule to the feedback, so that each feels like a "natural" extension of the other.

Less Is More

The more methods of feedback you use, the more intrusive the feedback is. An animation accompanied by a sound and a haptic buzz is far more attention getting than any of those alone. *The third principle for microinteractions feedback is to convey the most with the least.* Decide what message you wish to convey ("Downloading has begun") then determine what is the least amount of feedback you could provide to convey that message. The more important the feedback is, the more prominent (and multichannel) it should be (Figure 4-12).

Figure 4-12. In Cornerstone, the number of segments in the spinning activity wheel are equal to the number of processes happening in the background. (Courtesy Yusuf Miles and Little Big Details.)

The fourth principle of feedback is to use the overlooked as a means of message delivery. Many microinteractions contain conventional parts of any interface—as they should. These overlooked parts of the UI—scrollbars, cursors, progress bars, tooltips/hovers, etc.—can be used for feedback delivery. This way, nothing that isn't already there will get added to the screen, but it can communicate slightly more than is usual

(Figure 4-13). For example, a cursor could change color to gray if the user is rolling over an inactive button.

Figure 4-13. OS X Lion's cursor changes to tell you when you can't resize a window in a particular direction. (Courtesy Little Big Details.)

Feedback as a Personality-Delivery Mechanism

Unlike the more utilitarian trigger and any controls for the rules, feedback can be a means of creating a personality for your microinteraction—and for your product as a whole. Feedback can be the moment to inject a little edge or a touch of humor into your microinteraction (see Figures 4-14 and 4-15).

Figure 4-14. When there is a long upload time, Dropbox suggests you eat a candy bar while waiting. (Courtesy John Darke and Little Big Details.)

The reason you'd want to do that is that, as pointed out previously, feedback is for humans. We respond well to human responses to situations, even from machines. Humans anthropomorphize our products already, attributing them motivations and characteristics that they do not possess. Your laptop didn't deliberately crash and your phone isn't mad at you. Designers can use this human tendency to our advantage by deliberately adding personality to products. This works particularly well for microinteractions;

because of their brevity, moments of personality are more likely to be endearing, not intrusive or annoying.

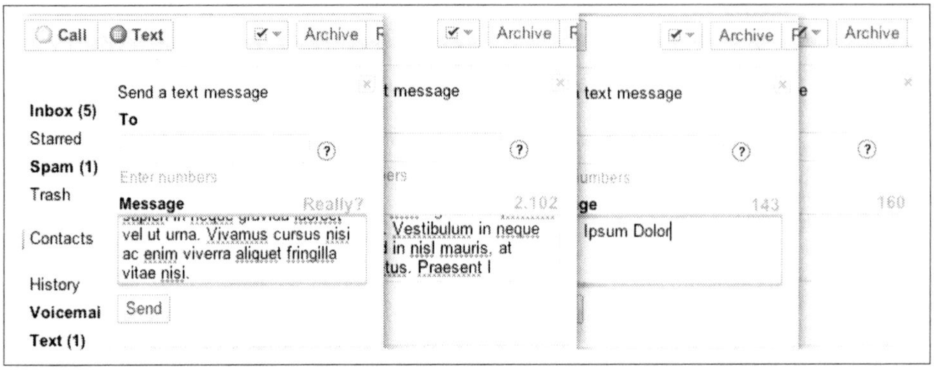

Figure 4-15. If your SMS gets too long, Google Voice stops counting characters and says, "Really?" (Courtesy Zoli Honig and Little Big Details.)

Take Apple's natural-language software agent Siri, for example. Siri easily could have been extremely utilitarian, and indeed, for most answers, "she"—it—is. But for questions with ambiguous or no possible factual responses like "What is the meaning of life?" Siri offers up responses such as "I don't know. But I think there's an app for that." In other words, what could have been potentially an error message ("I'm sorry. I can't answer that.") became something humorous and engaging. Indeed, errors or moments that could be frustrating for users such as a long download are the perfect place to show personality to relieve tension (see Figure 4-16).

We had a problem processing that request. Go to the IMDb homepage ›   Report this

500 ERROR   Error message! Why'd it have to be error messages?!

Indiana Jones, Raiders of the Lost Ark (1981)

Figure 4-16. For the Internet Movie Database (IMDb), the 500 error message is based on a movie quote. (Courtesy Factor.us and Little Big Details.)

Feedback with personality can, of course, be annoying if not done well or overdone. You probably don't want the login microinteraction giving you attitude every time you want to log in. And you might not want an app to chastise you if you forget your password: "Forgot your password again? FAIL!" What you should strive for is a *veneer of personality*. In the same way that being too human is creepy for robots—the so-called "uncanny valley"[8]—so too is too much personality detrimental for microinteractions. A little personality goes a long way (Figure 4-17). Making them too human-like not only sets expectations high—users will assume the microinteraction is smarter than it probably is—but can also come across as tone-deaf, creepy, or obnoxious.

Figure 4-17. Twitter for mobile acknowledges typing on a phone is difficult and may cause errors when logging in. (Courtesy Joris Bruijnzeels and Little Big Details.)

8. For a more complete definition and analysis of the uncanny valley, see "The Truth About Robotic's Uncanny Valley: Human-Like Robots and the Uncanny Valley," *Popular Mechanics*. January 20, 2010.

Speaking of creepy, while you want to collect and use behavioral data (and be transparent about what data you're collecting) to improve (or create) the microinteraction over time, being obvious (providing feedback) about collecting that data is a fast way to appear intrusive and predatory. You want people to be delighted with the personalization that data collection can provide, without being disgusted that data collection is going on.

Feedback Methods

We experience feedback through our five senses, but mostly through the three main ways we'll examine here: sight, hearing, and touch.

Visual

Let's face it: most feedback is visual. There's a reason for that, of course, in that we're often looking directly at what we're interacting with, so it is logical to make the feedback visual. Visual feedback can take many forms, from the blinking cursor that indicates where text should go, to text on a screen, to a glowing LED, to a transition between screens (Figure 4-18).

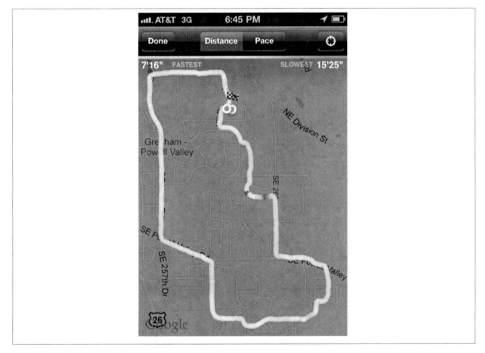

Figure 4-18. Nike+ App shows your slowest and fastest pace on its route map. (Courtesy David Knepprath and Little Big Details.)

Unless no screen or LED is available, assume that your default feedback is visual. Almost every user-initiated action (with the exception of actions users cannot do, such as clicking where there is no target) should be accompanied by visual feedback. With system-initiated triggers and rules, only some should have accompanying visual feedback—namely those that would require human intervention (e.g., an error indicator) or those that provide information a user may want to act upon (e.g., a badge indicating a new voicemail has arrived). Ask what the user needs to see to make a decision, then show that in as subtle a way as possible. Often what the user needs to be aware of is resources: time, effort, unread messages, etc. (Figure 4-19).

Figure 4-19. Navigon app changes its background when you go into a tunnel, as well as indicating how long before you reach the tunnel's end. (Courtesy Little Big Details.)

Don't show redundant visual feedback. For instance, never have a tooltip that mirrors the button label. Any visual feedback must add to clarity, not to clutter. Similarly, don't overdo a visual effect; the more frequent the feedback is, the less intrusive it should be. Don't make something blink unless it *must* be paid attention to (Figure 4-20).

Figure 4-20. Github uses a tooltip to show the absolute timestamp. (Courtesy Scott W. Bradley and Little Big Details.)

Visual feedback should also ideally occur near or at the point of user input. Don't have an error message appear at the top of the screen when the Submit button is on the bottom. As noted in Chapter 2, when we're attentive to something, our field of vision narrows. Anything outside of that field of vision can be overlooked (Figure 4-21). If you need to place visual feedback away from the locus of attention, adding movement to it (e.g., having it fade in) can draw attention to it.

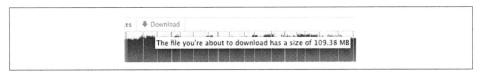

Figure 4-21. SoundCloud places the download size into a tooltip. This only works if the majority of users don't care about download size. (Courtesy David L. Miller and Little Big Details.)

Animation

Our brains respond powerfully to movement, so use animation sparingly. If you can do without animation, avoid it. Your microinteraction will be faster and less cognitively challenging without it. That being said, tiny, brief animations can add interest and convey meaning if done well (Figure 4-22).

Figure 4-22. On iPhones, the spinner next to the network speed spins faster or slower depending on the network speed. For instance, Edge networks spin slower than 3G ones. (Courtesy Little Big Details.)

The most important part of animation in microinteractions is that it indicates—accurately—a behavioral model of how the microinteraction works. Don't have a panel slide in from the left if it isn't going to slide out to the right, or if the user accesses it by swiping down. Animation for animation's sake is deadly. *The best animations communicate something to the user*: about the structure of the microinteraction, what to look at, what process is happening, etc.

Google's Android engineers Chet Haase and Romain Guy have devised a set of UI characteristics for animation (Figure 4-23). Animations should be:

Fast
Do not delay the activity

Smooth
Stuttering or choppy movements ruin the effect and make the microinteraction seem broken

Natural
They seemingly obey natural laws, such as gravity and inertia

Simple
Meaningful, understandable

Purposeful
Not just as eye candy

On this last point, designer and engineer Bill Scott outlines the reasons for using animation:[9]

- *Maintaining context while changing views.* Scrolling a list or a flipping through a carousel allows you see the previous and next items.

- *Explaining what just happened.* That poof of smoke means the item was deleted.

- *Showing relationships between objects.* For example, animating one item going into another at the end of a drag-and-drop.

- *Focusing attention.* As an item changes value, an animation can make that change more obvious.

- *Improving perceived performance.* Progress bars don't decrease the time needed for a download to happen, but they do make the time seem less grating.

---

9. "Anti-Pattern: Animation Gone Wild - Borders.com (*http://bit.ly/10dkku4*)," July 16, 2008.

Figure 4-23. In Android (Ice Cream Sandwich versions), the screen skews if you try to scroll past where there are items. (Courtesy Tony Mooch and Little Big Details.)

- *Creating an illusion of virtual space.* How (and where) panels slide in and out, for example. *Transitions* can be an important part of microinteraction animations as users move from one state to another, or from one mode to another. Transitions help give a sense of location and navigation, letting users know where they are and where they are going to.

- *Encouraging deeper engagement.* Interesting animations invite interaction.

Scott has a valuable rule for animation timing: make any animation half as long as you think it should be. And then possibly halve the timing again (as detailed in *Designing Web Interfaces*, O'Reilly). Animation should make the microinteraction more efficient (by illuminating the mental model or providing a means of directing attention) or at least *seem* more efficient, not less.

Messages

Designer Catriona Cornett tells of her experience updating the in-car Ford SYNC system. After putting the update on a USB drive to plug in to the car, she read these instructions:

> "Follow your printed out instructions exactly with your vehicle running. Approximately 60 seconds after you begin the installation, you will hear an 'Installation Complete' message. DO NOT REMOVE your USB drive or turn off your vehicle. You must wait an additional 4–18 minutes until you hear a second 'Installation Complete' message before you can remove your USB drive."
>
> OK, so, even though it will give me a message saying it's complete, it's really not, and if I didn't read this little note about the process, it makes it sound like I could cause some form of irreversible damage. Great.[10]

"Installation Complete" is clear enough as a message, in the above described case, unfortunately it's misleading. Any messages delivered as feedback to an action should—at a minimum—be accurate. As with instructional copy, any text as feedback should be short and clear. Avoid words like "error" and "warning" that provide no information and serve to only increase anxiety. Feedback text for any error messages should not only indicate what the error was, but also how to correct it. Ideally, it would even provide a mechanism for correcting the error alongside the message. For example, don't tell a user only that an entered password is wrong, provide the form field to re-enter it and/or a means of retrieving it (Figure 4-24).

While any text should be direct (and human), it's best to avoid using personal pronouns such as "you." "You entered the wrong password" is far more accusatory and off-putting than "Password incorrect." Likewise, avoid using "I," "me," or "my," as these are the uncanny valley of feedback copy. Although they can have human-like responses, microinteractions aren't human. Some voice interfaces like Siri can get away with using first-person pronouns, but in written form it can be jarring.

The ideal microinteraction text is measured in words, not lines, and certainly not paragraphs or even a single paragraph (Figure 4-25). Keep copy short and choose verbs carefully, focusing on actions that could or need to be taken: "Re-enter your password."

Audio

As noted in Chapter 2, sound can be a powerful cue that arrives quickly in our brains —more quickly than visual feedback. We're wired to respond to sound (and, as noted above, movement). Since it provides such a strong reaction, audio should be used

---

10. "UX principles in action: Feedback systems and Ford SYNC" (*http://bit.ly/ZIF1SV*), July 11, 2011.

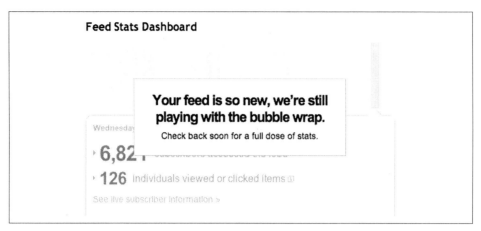

Figure 4-24. When you try to view your stats right away on Feedburner, you get this message. It would be better if it gave a more definite time to return.

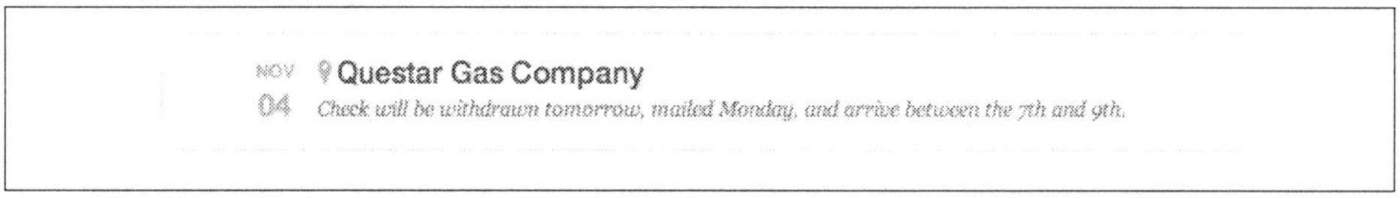

Figure 4-25. Banking service Simple explains in one pithy line exactly what is going to happen in the future. (Courtesy Little Big Details.)

sparingly. However, audio can be particularly useful on devices with no screens, or as part of microinteractions that work in the background when the user isn't fully paying attention to them. It can also be useful in situations where looking at a screen can be unsafe, such as while driving.

In general, there are two ways to use audible feedback: for emphasis and for alerts. Audio for emphasis is typically for reinforcing a user-initiated action, as a confirmation that what the user thought happened actually did. Clicking a button and hearing a click is an example. These are often combined with visual feedback, and audio combined with visuals has been shown to be more effective than visuals alone.[11] The other kind of audio feedback—alerts—are typically indicators of system-initiated actions: a process has ended, a condition has changed, or something is wrong. A voice telling you to turn left in a navigation app is an example of an audio alert.

Any audio cue for a microinteraction should pass the *Foghorn Test*: is this action important enough that users would want to become aware of it when they cannot see it?

---

11. Brown, Newsome, and Glinert, "An experiment into the use of auditory cues to reduce visual workload," 1989.

Even if you think the answer is yes, you should possibly provide a mechanism to turn the sound off.

Like other feedback, audio can be adjusted if there is an understanding of the context of use. Some HTC phones buzz and ring loudly in their user's pockets or purses (the phone knows it is there via sensor data) and diminish in volume as the user removes them. Some automobiles increase the volume of music to compensate as the engine gets louder. Similarly, if the user isn't in the room with a device (detected via a proximity sensor) or the noise in the room is loud (detected by a microphone), volume and pitch could increase. And sound cues could also turn on (or increase in volume) if the device knows you are in a situation where visual cues are compromised, such as while driving (detected via GPS).

Sound designer Karen Kaushansky also cautions designers to consider the "non-use-case" when designing audio: when does audio not make sense? Broadcasting a sound—particularly voices—into an empty room in the middle of the night can be both startling and annoying.[12]

Earcons

There are two kinds of audio feedback: earcons and words. Earcons—a play on the word "icons" ("eye-cons")—are short, distinct sounds meant to convey information.[13] The amount of information that earcons can convey is limited, however, and sometimes words are necessary. Words are recorded (spoken) or computer-generated text. Words are particularly useful for instructions or directions, although if your product has to be in many languages, localization of the text could be nontrivial. Speech is also much slower than earcons; what can be conveyed in a fraction of a second with an earcon could take several seconds in speech—a ping versus "You've got mail!"

Earcons are, by their very nature, abstract, so care should be taken to select a sound that could indicate the message being conveyed. For microinteractions, the best earcons are those that users (consciously or unconsciously) can relate to other sounds they have heard and make associations. For example, the click of a latch closing can be the earcon for the microinteraction ending, or an upward whoosh can accompany an item moving to the top of a list. Avoid earcons that are too shrill (except for critical warnings) or too soft ("Did I just hear that?"). As with animation, the best earcons are brief: under one second in duration, and usually a fraction of a second. One exception is an ambient sound to indicate an ongoing process, such as a drone to indicate a file being synced.

12. See "Guidelines for Designing with Audio," *Smashing Magazine* (*http://bit.ly/XLqBAz*).

13. Blattner, Meera M., Sumikawa, Denise A., and Greenberg, Robert M., "Earcons and Icons: Their Structure and Common Design Principles," Journal of Human-Computer Interaction, Volume 4, Issue 1, 1989.

Any earcon should also match the emotional content being conveyed. Is the feedback urgent or just utilitarian? A warning or an announcement? The qualities of the earcon (timbre, pitch, duration, volume) should match what is being communicated.

If you want your earcon to be iconic and memorable (a Signature Sound), it should contain two to four pitches (notes) played in succession.[14] As you don't necessarily want your microinteraction to be memorable, this trick should be used only once per microinteraction, if at all. Most microinteraction earcons should be a single-pitch sound, played once. Beware of playing any earcon in a loop, as even the softest, gentlest sound can be irritating played over and over and over.

Earcons should be unique to an action. Just as you want to avoid using the same visual feedback for different actions, you shouldn't use the same—or even similar-sounding —earcons for dissimilar events. This is especially true for alert sounds that could be triggered independent of user actions. If the user is looking away from (or isn't close to) the device, the user won't be sure of which action just happened.

Speech

If you're going to use words as audio feedback, keep the spoken message brief and clear. If there is a prompt for a response, make the choices clear, short, and few. Ideally with microinteractions, any voice responses would be "Yes" or "No," or at worst a single word. As noted in Chapter 3, microinteractions are the place for smart defaults, not multiple choice. Any word prompt should be at the end of the message. Use "To turn sound off, say yes" instead of "Say yes to turn sound off." Always end with the action.

With speech, your choice is to use actors to record the messages, or to use text-to-speech (TTS). Recorded messages have the advantage of feeling more human and can have more texture and nuance, although care has to be taken to make sure the actors convey the right message and tone via their inflections and pauses. The minus is that any time you change the message, it has to be rerecorded.

If the messages are dynamic (for example, turn-by-turn directions), TTS is probably your only option, as you would unlikely be able to record every street name. Although TTS has improved in recent years, it can still feel inhuman and impersonal, and some people actively dislike it, so use with care.

Haptics

Haptics, or as they are technically known, "vibrotactile feedback." Haptics are vibrations, usually generated by tiny motors, which can create a strong, tactile buzz or more delicate tremors that can simulate texture on flat surfaces. Compared to the decades of visual

---

14. See previous footnote, and Kerman, Joseph, *Listen*, Bedford/St. Martin's, 1980.

and audio feedback, haptics is relatively new, with the majority of people only having experienced it with the advent of pagers and mobile phones.

Haptics, since they are mostly felt (although the vibration can make noise against a hard surface like a tabletop), are best utilized on devices the user will be in close proximity to (by holding, touching, wearing, or carrying), although they can also be embedded in objects like furniture to enhance entertainment like movies and games. Faces and hands (particularly fingertips) are the most sensitive to haptics, while legs and torso are much less so.

Even more than vision and hearing, our sense of touch (technically our cutaneous sense) is limited. Not by our skin, which is extensive (although of varying sensitivity to touch), but by our brains. There are four kinds of fibers known as mechanoreceptors that convey cutaneous sense, each of which can detect different frequencies. The different mechanoreceptors engage in crosstalk with each other, the result of which determines what we can feel—which, as it turns out, isn't much. One researcher claims the amount of information we can get from touch is 1% that of hearing.[15] Most people can only easily detect three or four levels of vibration.[16] Thus, complex messages are not readily conveyed with haptics.

Luckily, complex messages are usually unnecessary with microinteractions. Haptics have three main uses for microinteraction feedback. The first is to enhance a physical action, such as by simulating the press of a button on a touchscreen, or by giving an added jolt when the ringer of your phone is turned off. The second (and currently most common) use of haptics is as an alert when audio isn't available or is undesirable. The vehicle-initiated vibration of the steering wheel to wake a sleepy driver is an example of this use. The third (and thus far rarest) use is to create an artificial texture or friction on surfaces such as touchscreens. This can be used to slow down scrolling, for instance.

Because of humans' limited ability to detect differences in haptics, they are currently best used in microinteractions for either subtle, ambient communication or for a disruptive alert. There's very little middle ground, except perhaps in specialty devices, like those for musicians and surgeons, where varying levels of haptics can provide more physical feedback while doing an action like making music or performing surgery.

15. R. T. Verrillo, A. J. Fraioli, and R. L. Smith, "Sensation magnitude of vibrotactile stimuli," *Perception & Psychophysics*, vol. 6, pp. 366–372, 1969.

16. Gill, John, "Guidelines for the design of accessible information and communication technology systems" (*http://bit.ly/11kpcQz*). Royal Institute of the Blind, 2004, and F. A. Geldard and C. E. Sherrick, "Princeton cutaneous research project, report no. 38," Princeton University, Princeton, NJ, 1974.

Feedback Rules

Feedback can also have its own set of rules that dictate its instantiation (Figure 4-26). Feedback rules define:

Contextual Changes
>   Does the feedback change based on the known context? For instance, if it is night, does the volume increase? Decrease?

Duration
>   How long does the feedback last? What dismisses it?

Intensity
>   How bright/fast/loud/vibrating is the effect? Is it ambient or noticeable? Does the intensity grow in time, or remain constant?

Repetition
>   Does the feedback repeat? How often? Does the effect remain forever, or just for a few seconds?

Figure 4-26. Foursquare makes a plea for help when you pull down too far to refresh. (Courtesy Tory Briggs.)

These rules can determine much of the character of the feedback.

If you don't want your users feeling cheated and putting their fists through the screen as they do with slot machines, look to your feedback. Make the rules understandable, and inform them of changes in state when appropriate. Make the feedback consistent, rewarding positive behavior.

Sometimes it's not just a piece of feedback that repeats, it's the whole microinteraction. In Chapter 5, next, we'll discuss how to use loops and modes to extend your microinteraction.

Summary

Understand what information the user needs to know and when. All feedback relies on this understanding.

Feedback is for understanding the rules of the microinteraction. Figure out which rules deserve feedback.

Determine what message you want to convey with feedback, then select the correct channel(s) for that message.

Look at context and see if the feedback can (or should) be altered by it.

Be human. Feedback can use a veneer of humanity to provide personality to the microinteraction.

Use preexisting UI elements to convey feedback messages. Add to what is already there if you can before adding another element.

Don't make feedback arbitrary. Link the feedback to the control and/or the resulting behavior.

Whenever possible, have visual feedback for every user-initiated action. Add sound and haptics for emphasis and alerts.

CHAPTER 5

Loops and Modes

On January 4, 2004, a 400-pound, six-wheeled, solar-powered robot landed on Mars, in the massive impact crater Gusev. The robot was the $400-million-dollar *Spirit* rover that had taken over a year to build. As Passport to Knowledge reported (*http://bit.ly/ Z9ewWT*), *Spirit* had just survived the six-month journey to the Red Planet and a perilous landing, including bouncing as high as a four-story building on first impact with the surface. The Jet Propulsion Laboratory (JPL) team that built and commanded the rover thought the worst was behind them. They were wrong.

Once the (literal) dust—red—had settled, *Spirit* began its mission of taking pictures and performing scientific experiments, rolling toward a nearby destination ("Sleepy Hollow"). But then on January 21, less than three weeks into the mission, something happened. NASA's Deep Space Network lost contact with *Spirit*.

At first, the rover's disappearance was blamed on a thunderstorm in Australia disrupting the network, but no, there was something wrong with *Spirit* itself. The next day, a transmission arrived from *Spirit*: a single beep that indicated the rover was still there, but that was all. This was seriously bad. If the problem was a critical hardware failure, the robot was dead and its mission was effectively over.

Trying a number of methods, JPL finally coaxed the rover to send diagnostic data, which it did on January 23. Much of the data was just repeated nonsense, but it did give them some insight into what was happening. The news wasn't good: higher internal temperature than was expected, and lower battery voltage. Normally, the rover's computer is only on five or six hours a day to save battery power and to prevent it from overheating, but the data showed the rover wasn't going into sleep mode, and thus burning battery power and overheating. If this condition continued, the rover would destroy itself. As Mark Adler, one of the tactical mission managers, put it, "What we had on our hands was one sick rover. *Spirit* had insomnia, a fever, was getting weaker all the time, was babbling incoherently, and was largely unresponsive to commands."

 Adler's gripping first-person account can be read in full in "Spirit Sol 18 Anomaly," by the Planetary Society Blog at this link (*http://bit.ly/11oJiJR*).

Frantic, the command team sent *Spirit* a `SHUTDWN_DMN_TIL` ("shutdown dammit until") command, which puts the rover to sleep. *Spirit* accepted the command and the JPL team breathed a sigh of relief. Just to make sure, they sent a beep to the rover; if *Spirit* was really asleep, it wouldn't respond.

It did.

Spirit wasn't responding to commands, and because the Earth was "setting" inside the crater, the JPL didn't have another chance to try something else until the next day. Meanwhile, *Spirit* was overheating and running out of power. Time was running out.

The JPL team regrouped to figure out what exactly was happening. They came up with a working theory: that *Spirit* was in fault mode, meaning it was trying to reboot itself after encountering a problem that it couldn't solve—basically just like all of us do with our gadgets when they become unresponsive. The problem was that *Spirit* seemed to be trapped in fault mode, rebooting itself over and over. It was encountering a problem *while* rebooting.

Later, it would be figured out the problem was with a software update that had happened while the rover was en route to Mars. During the update, a utility to delete the old software files was uploaded, but the upload failed and no one noticed—or else it was ignored. The result was that there was less file space available because it was being taken up by the older files. So when *Spirit* started running experiments and saving data, the file system overflowed. To try to fix it, *Spirit* rebooted itself. (This was what it was supposed to do.) The problem was that the reboot couldn't complete due to insufficient available file space, which *Spirit* tried to fix by rebooting. And thus an infinite loop of reboots was entered.[1]

The command team didn't know this at the time; they just guessed *Spirit* was repeatedly rebooting and had to figure out how to stop it before the rover was irreparably damaged. JPL suspected that, since the problem persisted through reboots, the issue was either the flash memory, the EEPROM, or a hardware fault. (If it had been hardware, the rover would be irreparable.) Fortunately, the rover engineers had anticipated problems with the flash memory and EEPROM, so they'd designed a way the rover could be booted without ever touching the flash memory: the radio that received commands from Earth could also execute a limited number of commands itself, one of which was telling the computer to reboot without using flash memory. The JPL team sent the command to the radio several times before it finally worked and the loop was broken. Relieved, JPL retrieved some data, and put *Spirit* into a long-overdue sleep.

Luckily, this story has a happy ending, in that *Spirit* returned to full operation on February 5, 2004, and continued operating for years, even though its solar panels were designed only to last three months and even after getting stuck in a sand trap for two years. The last successful communication with *Spirit* was in March 22, 2010—nearly seven years longer than JPL expected—and NASA officially ended *Spirit*'s mission (*http://1.usa.gov/11oJzMX*) on May 25, 2011 after "a stressful Martian winter without much sunlight. With inadequate energy to run its survival heaters, the rover likely experienced colder internal temperatures last year than in any of its prior six years on Mars." As of this writing (March 2013), *Spirit*'s twin rover, *Opportunity*, which arrived three weeks after *Spirit*, is still exploring the surface of Mars.

A mode, like *Spirit*'s fault mode, is a special part of an application in which the app operates differently than usual. Often, this means actions like pressing a key does something else when in a particular mode. A loop, like the reboot one *Spirit* was stuck in, is traditionally a command or series of commands that is repeated. (As we'll see, it's defined slightly differently for microinteractions.) As the near disaster with *Spirit* reveals, loops and modes can be tricky things, even for the conservative, thorough NASA.

Modes

A mode is a fork in the rules, and for microinteractions, modes should be used very, very sparingly. Most microinteractions should be mode-free, but sometimes they are necessary. The best reason to have a mode is when there is an infrequent action that would otherwise clutter the microinteraction's main purpose. One common mode is a settings mode, wherein the user specifies something about the microinteraction. When you're in settings mode, you're not usually performing the major task, just modifying

---

1. For the full details, see "The trouble with rover is revealed" by Ronald Wilson, *EE Times*, February 20, 2004.

it. It's separate from the rest of the interaction. Examples of this are in weather (see Figure 5-1) or stock market apps, when you select cities or stock ticker symbols to get data on them. You're not performing the main action of the microinteraction; it's a deviation in the rules that takes you away to do one subtask, then return.

Figure 5-1. An example of a mode from Apple's Weather App for iOS.

The reason to avoid modes in general is that they can cause errors, especially if the mode is just an invisible state the screen is in. Turning on an edit mode, for example, makes a once-familiar screen something the user has to relearn. An action, such as clicking an item, could do drastically different tasks: selecting the item in default mode, deleting it in delete mode. The fewer modes—and in microinteractions, there should be no more than one, and zero if possible—the less chance of users being confused about what mode they are in, and the less they have to learn about how the microinteraction works.

If you must have a mode, a good practice for microinteractions is to make it its own screen whenever possible (or whenever there is even a screen). (This is the one exception to the "don't make a screen for every rule" principle discussed in Chapter 3.) This will help reduce errors and frustration, because it will hopefully make it clearer to the user they are in a different mode, not just an unfamiliar state. A transition to the new mode—and back to the previous (default) mode—can be a useful cue here as well, indicating to the user they are going somewhere else to do something specific.

When a user goes to one mode and comes back to the previous mode, they expect the original mode to be in the same state as they left it, although perhaps any changes performed while in the other mode will be reflected in the default mode. When a user exits to a special mode and then returns to the main interaction, she expects the main interaction to be in the same state as she left it—with the addition of any changes made while in the special mode. For example, in a weather app, if I add another city in the Add a City mode, when I return to looking at weather data, I should see the new city there.

Spring-Loaded and One-off Modes

It's annoying to have to switch to a different mode to perform one simple action. Two variations of modes that could be used in microinteractions in addition to (or in place of) traditional modes are spring-loaded modes and one-off modes. With either of these variations, the user can't get trapped in an unknown mode.

Spring-loaded modes (sometimes called quasimodes[2]) are only active when a physical action such as pressing a key or holding down a mouse button is occurring. As soon as the action stops, so does the mode. The classic example is pressing the Shift key on your keyboard, which turns on caps lock mode, but only while pressing the Shift key. The Alt, Option, and Command keys also often turn on a spring-loaded mode.

The value of a spring-loaded mode is that the user seldom forgets that they are in a different mode, because they are doing something physical to make that mode possible, and it doesn't require switching to a different screen. The drawback is that it doesn't work well for actions that take some time to execute or require complex input.

For microinteractions, spring-loaded modes are best used sparingly, and probably mostly on devices and appliances. Pressing and holding a Start key can cause a reboot or reset, for example.

Spring-loaded modes can also be an invisible trigger that brings users to a microinteraction. Autofill in a search field is an example of this. Autofill only appears when there is text in the field, so it's a type of spring-loaded mode.

The same is mostly true with one-off modes. *One-off modes* are when a user initiates a mode that lasts for the duration of a single action, then the mode turns off. For example, double-tapping on text in iOS brings up its cut-and-paste features, which disappear

---

2. Quasimodes were introduced in the late Jef Raskin's seminal book *The Humane Interface* (Addison-Wesley Professional).

after one command has been selected. Newer versions of Microsoft Office have a so-called "minibar" of formatting tools that appears only when a user highlights some text. And in OmniGraffle, after a single use, a selected tool (such as the line tool) reverts back to its default state (the pointer). One-off modes are most useful for rapid task switching (as in OmniGraffle) or for contextual use (as in Office and iOS).

One-off modes can also be helpful for gestural and voice microinteractions. For example, in some voice interfaces, such as on the Xbox with Kinect, a command word (in this case "Xbox" being it), could be the trigger, which initiates a one-off mode in which another command could be issued. "Lights! Dim!" or "TV! Off!" (A fictional version of this is in *Star Trek*: "Computer, Locate Commander Riker!") Similarly, with gestural interfaces, one gesture such as a wave could trigger the microinteraction, putting it into one-off mode in which another gestural command could be issued. In both these cases, one-off modes prevent accidental triggering. In both these examples, the one-off mode would have to time out after a certain period of time, and for that, you need a loop.

Loops

A loop (in microinteraction parlance) is a cycle that repeats, usually for a set duration. The cycle can be microseconds, minutes, days, or even years. Loops are all about timing, determining the pace and the overall lifespan of the microinteraction. Although most microinteractions are generally short in duration, they or parts of them can repeat, and thus have a longer "life" than just a brief moment.

A loop is something indicated (directly or indirectly) via the rules. "Get data every 30 seconds" or "Run for three minutes, then stop" or "Send a reminder in 10 days" are all example indicators that a loop is involved.[3]

Styles of Loops

We're concerned with four kinds of loops:

Count-Controlled (For) Loop
This repeats *for* a set number of times before ending. For example, check if there is network connectivity 10 times before giving an error message.

Condition-Controlled (While) Loop
This repeats *while* a certain set of conditions is met. If the conditions change or end, so does the loop. If there is a network connection, check for new Twitter messages every minute.

---

3. Developers may take issue with this definition, as a traditional loop (in computer science terms) would not be employed to make this possible. Instead something like a "Wait" or "Sleep" command would likely be used.

Collection-Controlled Loop

Similar to a Count-Controlled loop, this loop runs through everything in a set, then stops. Example: for each unread email, add one to the unread counter.

Infinite Loop

A loop that begins and never ends until there is an error or someone shuts it down. As with the story of the *Spirit* rover, these are generally to be avoided, but a microinteraction like turning on a light basically starts an infinite loop: the light doesn't turn off again until the whole microinteraction is turned off or the light bulb burns out.

Additionally, there are two kinds of loops: open or closed. Microinteractions make use of both for different purposes. *Open loops* do not respond to feedback; they execute and end. ("Every day at 10pm, turn on a light.") *Closed loops* have a feedback mechanism built in and are thus self-adjusting. For example, a closed loop could be one that, while the car is running, checks the engine noise level and adjusts the car stereo volume accordingly.

As with the algorithms we discussed in Chapter 2, defining the parameters of loops can contribute mightily to the user experience. Too few cycles in a loop can make the experience feel rushed or intrusive; too long a loop could make the experience sluggish and nonresponsive. Figure 5-2 shows an example of a timing loop.

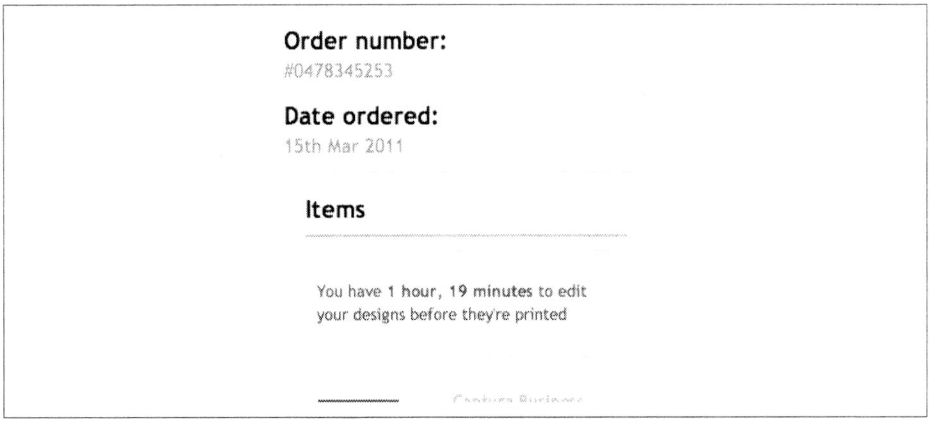

Order number:
#0478345253

Date ordered:
15th Mar 2011

Items

You have 1 hour, 19 minutes to edit
your designs before they're printed

Figure 5-2. Moo starts a timing loop after an order has been placed, to show users how long they have to edit a recently placed order. (Courtesy Matt Donovan and Little Big Details.)

Loops can be used to make sure an action doesn't go on too long or end a process or even the entire microinteraction. This could be done for security reasons, for instance when a banking site automatically logs you out after a few minutes of inactivity. This kind of automatic ending can be annoying, so use with care (Figure 5-3).

Figure 5-3. If a user clicks too many Add Friend buttons too quickly, Facebook gives the user a warning. (Courtesy Alfie Flores Nollora and Little Big Details.)

Loops can be used to recognize behavior as well. For example, if a user has paused at one part of the microinteraction for too long, the microinteraction could prompt them with help (Figure 5-4).

Figure 5-4. If a video has been buffering for too long, the TED site offers users the option to download it for later. (Courtesy Justin Dorfman and Little Big Details.)

Sometimes just the repeating (an open loop) is enough. But the most powerful loops are those that take place over long durations and/or are closed loops that adapt over time to behavioral feedback. These are long loops.

Long Loops

"Something in design has gone wrong when objects don't mature in a way that makes them more desirable."

—Deyan Sudjic

Let's talk about hammers for a moment. Hammers, like most tools, are very good for a few discreet activities—just like microinteractions. In the case of hammers, this is pounding or removing nails, as well as occasionally smashing something. But microinteractions aren't hammers. They can have memory. They can use data. They can loop, sometimes endlessly. When designing microinteractions, you can use what I'm calling long loops and focus not only on doing an individual task, but also on a longer timescale. What can be done to make the microinteraction better the second time it's used? The tenth? The ten thousandth? Figures 5-5 and 5-6 are examples of microinteractions that have undergone recent improvements.

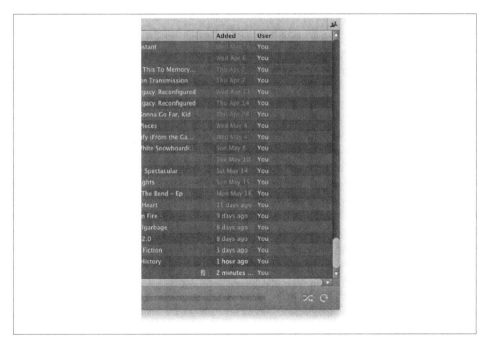

Figure 5-5. The songs in the "Added" column on Spotify fade over time. (Courtesy Jorge Nohara and Little Big Details.)

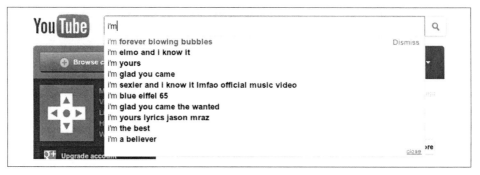

Figure 5-6. YouTube indicates recently made searches in purple. (Courtesy Davide Dettori and Little Big Details.)

Loops can deliver what design strategist and CEO of design consultancy Adaptive Path Brandon Schauer calls The Long Wow (*http://bit.ly/YzYXE6*). The Long Wow is about delivering new experiences or features over time instead of all at once, and by doing so building customer loyalty (see Figures 5-7 and 5-8). For the purpose of microinteractions, The Long Wow is about adapting the microinteraction over time so that it feels customized or even brand-new. This requires a long loop, perhaps one that lasts the duration of the device the microinteraction is contained in or even beyond, if behavioral data can be stored remotely or transferred to a new device.

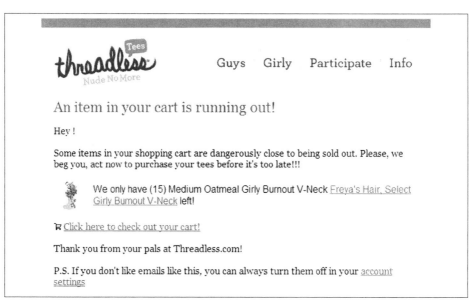

Figure 5-7. Threadless sends users an email when items in their cart are about to sell out. (Courtesy Little Big Details.)

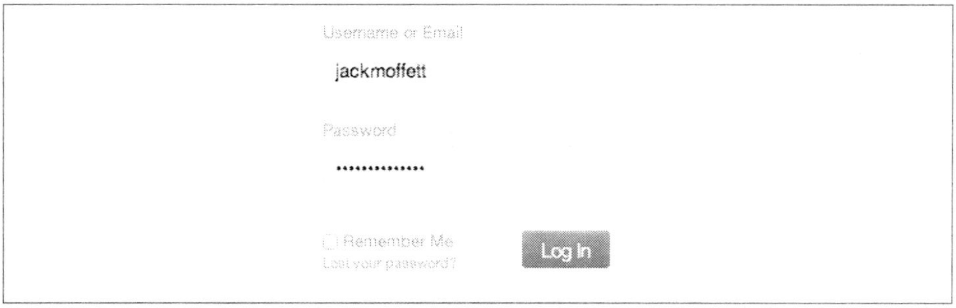
Username or Email
jackmoffett
Password
Remember Me
Lost your password?
Log In

Figure 5-8. Remember Me is the great broken loop of the Internet. What even happens when you check the box? Does it automatically log you in? (Unlikely.) Most times, it doesn't even remember you checked the box, leaving it unchecked. (Courtesy Jack Moffett.)

One use of these long loops is to extend the microinteraction far beyond a single instance of use. A weekly reminder of items placed on a wish list is one example, or the "Remember Me" checkbox that no website seems to remember is another. When a user returns to the microinteraction, ideally there is some memory of previous use. A user who likes to play her music loud may have different volume settings than someone who doesn't (Figure 5-9).

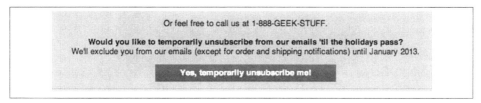

Or feel free to call us at 1-888-GEEK-STUFF.
Would you like to temporarily unsubscribe from our emails 'til the holidays pass?
We'll exclude you from our emails (except for order and shipping notifications) until January 2013.
Yes, temporarily unsubscribe me!

Figure 5-9. ThinkGeek allows users to temporarily unsubscribe while the holidays are ongoing. (Courtesy Kayle Armstrong and Little Big Details.)

Progressive disclosure or reduction

Another use of long loops is *progressive disclosure* over long periods of time. As users become used to a product, they don't need as much handholding, and instead can be treated as a more skilled user. For example, shortcuts could be added to a microinteraction after it's been used a few times, or more advanced features added.

Another option is *progressive reduction (http://bit.ly/17x4pLM)*, where the microinteraction becomes simpler over time, as the user becomes skilled and doesn't need items such as labels for guidance (see Figure 5-10 for an example). However, care must be taken; if the user doesn't engage with the product for a while, the microinteraction might have to become more robust and obvious again. The benefit to users is a cleaner interface, one that rewards and makes use of a user's familiarity with a product.

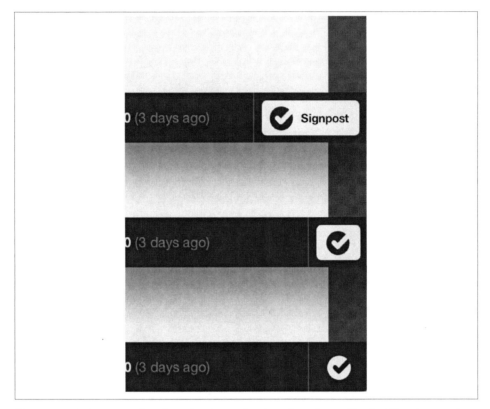

Figure 5-10. An example of progressive reduction from LayerVault. The signpost button's default is a large icon with a label. As the user becomes proficient, the label disappears. And eventually for experienced users, the button is de-emphasized altogether. (Courtesy LayerVault.)

As the near-disastrous story of the *Spirit* rover on Mars reminds us, loops and modes can be tricky to implement and maintain. However, their use can make a microinteraction cleaner (by moving infrequent actions like settings to a mode) and richer, by having the microinteraction adapt to use over time.

This completes the structure of microinteractions. Now it's time to put everything together that we've learned.

Summary

Only have a mode when there is an infrequent action that might otherwise clutter the microinteraction.

If you must have a mode, make it its own screen when possible.

For rapid actions, consider using a spring-loaded or one-off mode instead of a traditional mode.

Use loops to extend the life of a microinteraction.

Carefully consider the parameters of loops to ensure the best user experience.

Use long loops to give the microinteraction memory or to progressively disclose or reduce aspects of the microinteraction over time.

CHAPTER 6

Putting It All Together

TRIGGER   RULES   FEEDBACK   LOOPS & MODES

On a cold Boston night in February 2008, Leah Busque and her husband realized their dog Kobe was out of dog food. They were headed out to dinner and a cab was even on its way, but the dog needed to be fed. She thought, "Wouldn't it be nice to go somewhere online and say, 'We need dog food,' name a price we'd be willing to pay, and find someone in our neighborhood, maybe at the store that very moment, who could help us?" Before the cab had even arrived, she'd bought the domain name RunMyErrand.com.[1]

RunMyErrand eventually became the startup TaskRabbit, with Busque as its founder and CEO. TaskRabbit lets people locally outsource the small chores they don't want to do like donating old clothes or buying dog food. By 2011, TaskRabbit had millions in funding, 35 employees, and was generating $4 million USD in business every month.

At the heart of TaskRabbit is a microinteraction: telling potential "TaskRabbits" what task needs doing so that the TaskRabbits can bid on the fee for doing it. Specifying the task that needs to be done is the microinteraction. The entire service rests on this one crucial, yet potentially unexciting, step. At first, this microinteraction was a very text-heavy form, where users would have to write out their tasks in some detail (see Figure 6-1). But in 2011, after the team had designed their simpler mobile app, they realized there was a better way: by making a set of Smart Defaults, Bringing the Data

---

1. As told to Alyson Shontell in "Founder Q&A: Make A Boatload Of Money Doing Your Neighbor's Chores On TaskRabbit," *Business Insider*, October 27, 2011.

Forward, and breaking the task up into chunks. As detailed in "TaskRabbit Task posting forms" (*http://bit.ly/178y67D*), then director of UX Sarah Harrison explained: "As time went on, we got more data about our Tasks, our software got more sophisticated, and we were able to categorize Tasks into main Task types. This allowed us to create specific forms for common Task types, simplifying by asking for relevant details, setting smart defaults, and hiding irrelevant questions."

Figure 6-1. An early version of the TaskRabbit task-posting form. (Courtesy Sarah Harrison.)

The result is the (admittedly large) microinteraction in Figures 6-2 and 6-3. The user only has to pick a main task (Figure 6-2), then the next step of the microinteraction (Figure 6-3) is tailored based on that main task. Users were delighted (*http://bit.ly/13mDsK9*). "They made the entire task a no-brainer," said one. "They answer all the questions I have before I even ask them." This is the sign of a great microinteraction (Figure 6-4).

Figure 6-2. Step 1 of the redesigned TaskRabbit task microinteraction. (Courtesy Sarah Harrison.)

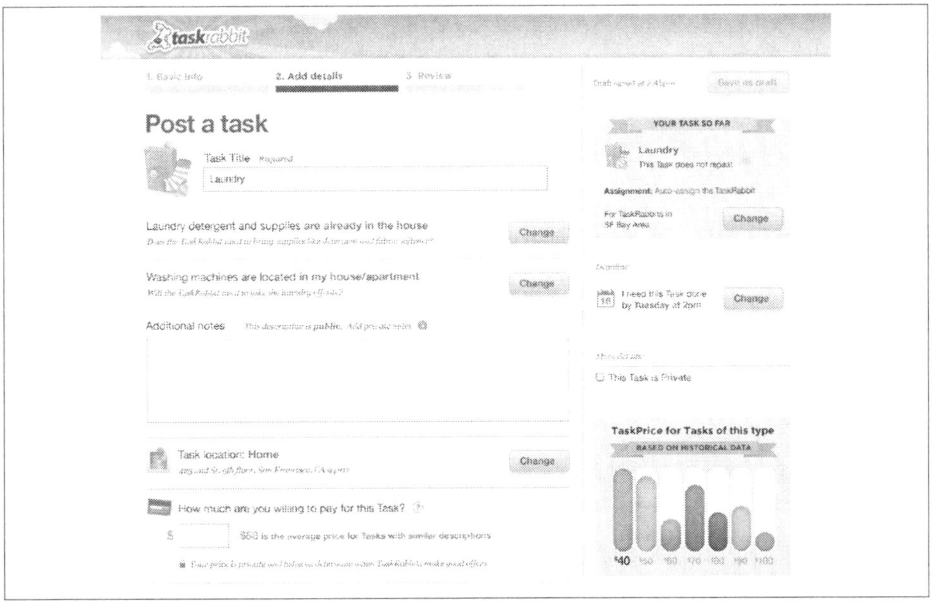

Figure 6-3. Step 2 of the form. Once the user picks a main task, the rest of the microinteraction is customized around it. (Courtesy Sarah Harrison.)

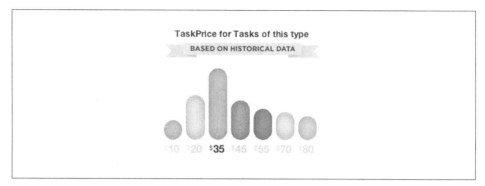

Figure 6-4. TaskRabbit brings the data forward here, answering the question, "How much should I offer?" (Courtesy Rishi Shah.)

In this chapter, we're going to put everything we've discussed together to make three example microinteractions: a mobile app for setting an alarm, a web widget for a shared playlist, and the control panel for a dishwasher.

Example 1: Mobile App

In this first example, we're going to look at an iPhone mobile app for setting an alarm. The microinteraction here is the entire app; all the app does is allow the user to set a time for an alarm to go off.

The first thing to think about is what the goal is: it's to be alerted (usually woken up) at a particular time. It's not to *set an alarm*: that's just a rule. So let's write out the rules we know we need at this point:

1. User selects a time for an alarm to go off.
2. The alarm goes off at the specified time.
3. The user turns off the alarm.

We'll fill out the rules more later. Let's now look at the trigger.

Since we've said the microinteraction is an iPhone app, the trigger is a given: it will be a standard icon that lives on the iPhone home screens. Since that's solved for us, let's see if we can *Bring the Data Forward* in any way.

What is the one piece of information that users would like to see before starting the microinteraction? In this case, it's whether or not an alarm has been set, and what time the alarm is set for. The mechanism Apple has for showing information inside an app are badges. Here we run into a snag. In another OS, like Windows Mobile using live tiles, we might be able to indicate in text and time whether there is an alarm and what time it's set for, but as of this writing (March 2013) with iOS 6, only numbers are allowed in iOS badges, and only four of them at that. So what do we do? If the alarm was set to 6:30 you could possibly do a badge that was 630, but what if the alarm was 12:30? Does 1230 convey the message? This is an atypical use of badges, which are normally for indicators such as unread messages, so that gives us pause. Also, if we do a badge that indicates the time, we're limiting ourselves to only one alarm; you can't show multiple alarm times given these constraints! This isn't necessarily a bad thing: only one alarm makes the rules much simpler. There is a way around showing multiple times in a badge, in that you would only show the *next* alarm in the badge. But this too could cause confusion, and confusion is the enemy of microinteractions. When in doubt, make it simpler. So until this constraint is changed (if ever) or we put our app on a different platform, the only data we'll bring forward is the number of alarms set and active. It's not as useful as knowing the time, but there is still some value in knowing at a glance if an alarm is set.

Our trigger needs a label, which in this case is the name of our app. Let's call it AlarmD.

What happens when AlarmD is triggered? The app launches, but then what does it show? If the goal is to be alerted at a particular time, it should either be showing when the alarm(s) are going to go off, or else prompting the user to set an alarm.

At this point, we should pause and ask what we know about the user so that we *Don't Start from Zero*. We know what platform the user is on and what device, so we also know what sensors are available to us (camera, microphone, accelerometer, compass). We know the time (obviously) and the location. If the app has been used before, we could know what previous alarms had been set, and how often. Does the user set the same alarm(s) every day, or just every weekday? We might also know what happened once those alarms went off: did the user press snooze at all? If so, for how many times? Let's add in some rules to account for some of this data:

1. If the user has set the same alarm for three days in a row and the alarm isn't set, prompt to set the same alarm when AlarmD is launched. If the user does set the prompted time, prompt whenever launched until the user does not select, then reset.

2. If the country the phone is in uses 24-hour format, use that.

3. Display any set alarms. Show the time until it goes off (e.g., "8 hours away").

4. User selects a time for an alarm to go off.

5. The alarm goes off at the specified time.

6. If the user presses the snooze button, repeat the alarm in five minutes. All subsequent snoozes come one minute earlier until they are one minute apart.

7. If after a week of use, the user has never pressed snooze, remove it from the alert.

8. The user turns off the alarm.

Notice there is already a *long loop* in there ("three days in a row") that engages a *system trigger* as well as some shorter loops (the snooze countdown). The display of "8 hours away" is a way to *Prevent Human Error* for setting an alarm too far in the future, by selecting P.M. instead of A.M., for example. The removal of the snooze button, while limiting options, could be controversial. We might need to be able to restore it via a setting somewhere. If our app weren't on iOS, we could do some other tricks with snooze, like make the alarm louder each time the alarm goes off after a snooze, but iOS doesn't allow apps to control the overall volume, so we're stuck with that constraint.

Next, let's take a look at the controls. The user has to be able to set an alarm, cancel an alarm, turn off an alarm, and snooze. These will all need visible controls of some sort in the UI, unless any of them could be hidden under a multitouch gesture. Almost all of them except for snooze are essential, and with snooze, you have users who are half asleep, so you cannot expect them to perform anything more complex than tapping a button. Setting an alarm time is the most complicated of these; everything else can be done via simple button taps. Setting the time could be done in various ways: using the built-in tumblers (as Apple's Clock app does) or via a custom control, such as selecting a time on an analog clock.

This is where we should pause and consider whether we want setting the alarm time to be a Signature Moment for the microinteraction, or just accomplished quickly. Since there are about 1,000 alarm apps on the market, setting the alarm might be a good place to do something custom and interesting. I've always been a fan of those old-fashioned train tickers, so this app will make use of them. Since, honestly, who needs to set an alarm for particular minutes, the minutes flipper will move in five-minute increments. *Optimize for what most people do most of the time.*

What will really make this custom control come to life is the feedback while adjusting it. It has to have a very satisfying clack as the tiles flip, and the way the tiles visually flip has to look like they obey gravity. Another important piece of feedback is the alarm itself. You could let users use the standard iPhone sounds or pick songs from their iTunes library, but a default, custom sound would be memorable here. Other places for custom sounds would be when canceling an alarm or when turning it off: something like a very definitive mechanical click, such as those when turning off a gas stove. Perhaps the alarm itself fades away instead of an abrupt cutting off as well.

The last thing to consider are loops and modes. An obvious mode here would be the setting of the alarm time, although since it's a single action, it could probably be accomplished in an One-off mode: tap it from a list of alarms, it opens up, the user sets the alarm, and it closes. A more traditional mode would be Settings, if we wanted to give users an option to set actions like the duration of snooze. I would advocate for not having settings. Make the defaults good enough to ship—at least in the first release.

As far as loops go, there are several. The alarm is several kinds of loops at once: the snooze is a count-controlled loop (make the alarm go off in five minutes, then four, then three, etc.) that turns into a condition-controlled loop (have the alarm go off once a minute). In fact, the whole alarm is one long condition-controlled loop, as the alarm goes off once the alarm time (the condition) is met, and continues to go off until manually stopped. Of course, we could—and probably should—put in a timer in the rules, so that if no one turns the alarm off for, say, 10 minutes, the alarm turns itself off.

Once again, the platform constrains us from using loops to their full potential. One nice addition would be for the app, two minutes before the alarm goes off, to check the light in the room via the phone camera. Then, if the room is dark, over the next two minutes gradually increase the light coming from the phone so that when the alarm does go off, the room is brighter. But on iOS, an app can't open itself. (There's certainly good reason behind this system rule, as it could be easily abused.) Only an alert can appear, which isn't even close to the same thing.

There are some long loops built in: the prompt for an alarm the user does repeatedly, and the hiding of the snooze button. One thing we (deliberately) didn't include is a way for the user to create a repeating alarm—that is, create their own loop. This adds a lot of complexity to the app, some of which we've moved to the microinteraction itself in the form of the initial long loop that checks to see if the user has set the same alarm repeatedly. We could add more nuance to the loop, to check to see if it is a weekday or a weekend and prompt accordingly, but to keep the rule simple, let's end there.

So there we have our first example of a microinteraction designed using the principles outlined in this book. Let's try another.

Example 2: Online Shared Playlist

The second example we're going to use is for an online music service (albeit fake). Let's say that as part of this music service's offerings, there is a shared playlist, where users and their friends can drop songs for each other. Let's also assume the service is sophisticated enough that you can use songs from other services or even a desktop app like iTunes. And finally, let's say our playlist lives among other microinteractions like adding friends and playing music.

We can start with the goal. The reason people would want to use this microinteraction is twofold: to discover new music and to share music. Of course, the secret motivations to use this microinteraction might be to tell friends your emotional state or to demonstrate how good your musical taste is. Underlying motivations are important, too.

Let's sketch out the basic rules first:

1. If a new song arrives, add it to the playlist.

2. The user can add a song to the playlist.

3. New songs are added to the end of the playlist.

Our microinteraction has two triggers: adding a song (a *manual trigger*), and a friend adding a song remotely (a *system trigger*). Let's talk about manual first. If we assume there is a visual display of the songs in the playlist, how do users know they can add a song to it? Since you can add songs from anywhere and the system is smart enough to find a version of the song everyone can listen to, being able to drag a song to the playlist seems like one way to do that. Making that discoverable might mean putting an empty slot at the top of the playlist, saying Drop a Song Here. We can change the label after the user has successfully put a song in the playlist, to something like "What are you listening to?" Perhaps we could even rotate the label options occasionally, prompting the user with labels such as "What's today's tune?" or "What does today sound like?"

Are there other manual triggers? If our music service has a menu bar, you could put a menu item there: Add to Shared Playlist, although that would only work with selected songs from within the service itself, except if there was nothing selected, we opened a dialog box for users to search for a (music) file. It seems clunky—and too much like a chore—for what's supposed to be a fun microinteraction. So let's keep Add to Playlist as a menu item, but only for selected items from within the service. For anything outside the service, it has to be dragged to the playlist. Let's also add a key command so frequent users can just select a song and use the command to add without fumbling around with menus or drag-and-drop.

We could also allow users to add songs by typing in a song title (and perhaps an artist name). But the more different kinds of triggers we have, the more complicated the microinteraction becomes. And besides, typing a song isn't really a very standard way to add a song to a playlist.

Adding a song to the playlist, or especially when a song appears from a friend, is a great place for some feedback, particularly some animation. The whole playlist should slide down one slot, and the new song drops in from the top, sliding in with a musical *plink*. Since it's an app about music, audible feedback makes some sense.

There is also the system trigger of your friends adding songs to the playlist. If you have the browser tab open to the service, you'll certainly see (and hear) the song arrive. But if you don't, it could be fun to change the browser tab slightly, just as an indicator something has happened. Let's make our "badge" a musical note with a smile inside it. We'll call it Notesy.

When the user does drag a song into the playlist, it might take a while for the system to match the song. We could just use a regular spinning icon, but why? Feedback is a place to add some personality. We'll *Use the Overlooked* and use the loader to make use of Notesy again. We can have Notesy "looking around" for a match, then smiling as some are found.

The system might have to offer multiple choices if there are variations or it's unsure. If there is only one match, and/or it matches both Artist and Song Name exactly, it should add the song directly to the playlist. Otherwise, it should offer possible matches. Presenting possible matches is where an *algorithm* comes into play. Since we don't want to overwhelm the user, we'll present no more than three possible matches for the song. Since it is more likely that the artist name will be correct than the song title, we can use that as an ordering factor in our algorithm: matches from that artist are first. If none of the three are correct, we can provide a mechanism to go get three more selections. If it can't find any matches, Notesy can appear and look sad.

At this point, we could ask whether or not users can delete songs from the shared playlist. Let's assume no, since in the worst case, users can always use the controls to skip over any tracks they don't like. Let's also assume that users can't rearrange songs in the playlist. We might find in testing or after launch that these are deal-breakers for adopting and using the service, but for now, it keeps our rules simpler.

Let's see what the rules look like now:

1. If a new song arrives, add it to the playlist. Show Notesy in the browser tab.

2. The user can add a song to the playlist by dragging it to the top of the playlist or by selecting a song and using the Add to Playlist menu item or by using a key command.

3. When new songs are added, search for a match. If matches are found, show them in groups of three and let the user select the correct one. If (or when) there is no match, show sad Notesy.

4. New songs are added to the end (top) of the playlist ordered by the time they are added.

Is there any way to get more depth from our microinteraction? What data is worth bringing forward? Well, it's certainly nice to know whose song is in the playlist and when it was added. Playlist duration and the number of songs in it are also useful tidbits. Being able to send a brief comment to the song adder about that particular song ("Not another '80s song!") would also be a nice microinteraction to attach here as well.

Adding a long loop to encourage users to contribute songs would be a way to encourage engagement. You could show the last day/time the user contributed, just as a mild reminder, or do some actual nagging via the dropbox label: "Feed me!"

How does the microinteraction end? It really doesn't as long as the user is logged in to the service, although we should probably put a cap on the number of songs in the playlist before a song drops off. Thirty songs seems reasonable.

And so ends this microinteraction. The next example moves us into the world of microinteraction devices.

Example 3: Dishwasher Control Panel

For our last example, we're going to design a low-cost dishwasher control panel—but with the added challenge of the dishwasher being screenless. Let's assume this very basic dishwasher has a speaker for sound and several settings for different washing cycles. Let's also assume we know what cycles most users need and want, and that this is a small number of cycle options—let's say four.

The goal for dishwashing is to clean dishes, glasses, and silverware. The basic rules are these:

1. The user loads the dishes and detergent into the dishwasher, then shuts the dishwasher door.
2. The user selects the washing cycle and turns on the dishwasher.
3. The dishwasher washes the dishes.

The trigger is so important here that we'll revisit it in a moment. First, let's figure out what we know so we *Don't Start from Zero*. We should be able to know time (duration), the last setting the user selected, and historic data on what the user has selected and when. Since this is a low-cost dishwasher, other sensors (except perhaps those inside the device) are probably unlikely. It's a very dumb appliance. We might not be starting from zero, but we're barely at one.

The pieces of data that we can bring forward are whether or not the dishwasher is running, where it is in the cycle, and how long until it's done. Most people probably don't care where the dishwasher is in the cycle, except to know when the dishes will be done. Since we have no screen, we'll have to come up with other feedback to indicate this. Perhaps we'll be able to *Use the Overlooked*.

So let's figure out the controls. We know we have (at least) two possible controls: turning the dishwasher on and setting the washing cycle. Turning the dishwasher on could easily be a button. And each washing cycle could also be a button. This would certainly be operationally simple: one button for everything, with perhaps an LED on or around the button to indicate what cycle has been selected and another on or around the on button to indicate the dishwasher is in operation. This set of controls doesn't really help us *Bring the Data Forward* though. We'd have to add in another kind of display to indicate when the dishes will be done—perhaps a thin strip of LEDs that are lit at the beginning and extinguish as the cycles complete.

Another way to do the controls would be as a dial, similar to what washing machines have. Users turn the dial to the setting they want, then pull the dial out or push in to start. The dial would move as it goes through cycles until it stops. As an added bonus we could use the seam between the dial and the case or even inside the dial as an LED timer. A dial would certainly be more visually simple than a row of buttons.

However, dials are often ugly, and although our dishwasher is low-cost, we don't want it to be ugly. Dials also protrude, and on a dishwasher, you might want a flatter surface so people don't bump into a dial. And, unlike a washing machine where users may care about where the machine is in the cycle, the data users really value with a dishwasher is when the dishwasher will be done, not the cycles. *Don't show feedback for what the user doesn't care about.* So let's do a row of buttons—perhaps nice capacitive buttons—one for each cycle, lined up from longest duration (Pots and Pans) on the left to the shortest (Quick Rinse) on the right, followed by (although separated from the cycles) a Start button. On the buttons: a label with the cycle name (or Start). Underneath the cycle buttons let's put our thin strip of LEDs.

Let's now look at our microinteraction as a sentence—both to make sure it makes sense and to figure out where the *nouns* and *verbs* are. The User selects a Cycle Button that turns on the LED Strip, and then presses the Start button that starts the countdown on the LED Strip. Examining our microinteraction nouns, each button has two possible states: selected or not. Objects that look the same should act the same, so let's make a soft glow around each when selected, although perhaps a different color for the cycles than for the start. Each cycle could have its own color, but that's probably overkill. Using the principle of *Emphasize the Next Action*, the Start button should also draw attention to itself once a cycle button has been pushed because that is the next action a user has to take in the process.

Since the LED is counting down the time until the dishwasher stops (it's a *Count-Controlled loop*), its color should probably match that of the Start button. Our LED progress bar could be broken up into segments, each roughly 15 minutes—we probably don't know exact time, because a cycle like Auto Wash makes use of internal sensors to determine how long to wash the dishes. If the water is still dirty, it will run another cycle.

A rule and crucial piece of feedback we're missing is what happens when the dishwasher is done. After all, the goal is to have clean dishes, and the user wants to know when that goal is accomplished. We have a speaker, so one means of feedback could be a Signature Sound (a "Ta da!") on finishing. But you can't count on the user being within hearing range, and you definitely do not want to repeat the sound until the dishwasher is opened or reset. (Hey, what about Reset? We'll get to that in a moment.) So let's make the Start button and LED Strip red until the dishwashing cycle ends, then the LED strip turns off and the Start button glows green (or perhaps blue, so it's easier read by the color blind) to indicate the dishes are now clean. So the Start button now has four states: Off, Push Me, Working, and Clean. Once the dishwasher is opened, it should reset itself to Off.

Oh, and let's talk about Reset. There may be times our simple sentence doesn't work as smoothly as we like. Users might open the dishwasher in the middle of the cycle—and leave it open. We could be *Poka-Yoke* and simply lock the dishwasher when it was running, but that seems overly restrictive. Thus, we need some rules around opening the dishwasher and a means to reset the dishwasher as well. We could have a separate button for reset, although since it would work differently than the other buttons (because it's not a toggle—you can't select it; there is no selected state) we'd have to have a different kind of button, since we don't want an object that looks the same but acts differently. Another way is to simply use a *Spring-Loaded mode* on the Start button. Pressing and holding the Start button triggers a reset. I like that solution better, if for no other reason than it removes a button that would be used infrequently. We're using fewer nouns to do more verbs. But the reset action isn't particularly discoverable, so we probably need a label underneath: Hold to Reset. We might have to add a loop to do an automatic reset if the door is left open for too long.

The only remaining question is if we can use *Don't Start from Zero*. We can collect data about the last cycle used and when, but it's unclear if any of this information would actually be helpful. Yes, we could have the dishwasher display the last cycle the user requested, and with four options, this might save the user pressing the cycle button 25% of the time (if all the cycles are used equally, which is unlikely). We could put a long loop in there to see if we can't save a button press occasionally, but it might make the microinteraction feel inconsistent: sometimes a cycle would light up automatically, sometimes not. Either we have to have it on the last cycle selected, or nothing at all.

Here are our final rules, once everything is put together:

1. The user loads the dishes and detergent into the dishwasher, then shuts the dishwasher door.

2. Unless Reset has been used, the last cycle used and accompanied estimated duration on the Progress Bar should be lit up and the Start button should pulse (Push Me state) until pressed.

3. The user can change the washing cycle, which changes the duration on the Progress Bar.

4. The user presses the Start button. The Start button glows red (Working).

5. The dishwasher starts washing the dishes. The LED progress bar counts down.

6. If the dishwasher is opened, pause the cycle. When re-closed, resume. If the door remains open for more than an hour, reset.

7. When the dishwasher is done, the cycle button and progress indicator turn off. The Start button glows green.

8. When the dishwasher door is opened, the Start button switches to off.

9. At any time, if the user presses and holds the Start button for three seconds, the microinteraction resets and dishwashing stops. All buttons go to the off state and the Progress Bar is cleared.

We never did make use of the speaker we have available for additional feedback. (If this was a higher-end appliance, we could possibly also make use of haptics, too.) We certainly have several moments to reinforce actions with sound. Especially if we're using capacitive buttons, we could use sound to create button-press clicks. Pressing Start could certainly be a time to use an earcon for a Signature Sound. Although it seems obvious to create an earcon for when dishwashing has ended, broadcasting it in the middle of the night into an empty room could be anxiety-producing. If we were designing a more expensive dishwasher that could algorithmically check the time (via the network), the brightness of the room (via light sensor), and maybe even activity in the room (via motion sensor) it could only broadcast its earcon when it suspects people are awake and nearby. But alas, not on this model.

And so ends our example microinteractions. Hopefully, this provides a sense of how the structure and principles outlined in this book can be brought together to create well-crafted microinteractions.

Prototyping and Documenting Microinteractions

The reason to document and prototype any product is to communicate an idea: this is how it could (or should) work. With microinteractions, the most difficult idea to convey is the overall flow: how all the pieces fit together. It's this overall flow that communicates how the microinteraction should *feel*.

There are a number of ways to accomplish this goal:

Prototype on the platform.
> If you have technical skills or access to them, prototyping on the platform where the microinteraction will live is probably the best way to really understand how the microinteraction will work. However, it is also likely the most time-consuming way as well.

Make a movie.
> Movies are fast ways to convey timing and flow. They can be actual movies with video (see Figure 6-5) and a post-production tool such as AfterEffects, or they can be animations, such as those created with HTML5.

Create frame-by-frame storyboards.
> You can also show the microinteraction as a set of linked storyboards (see Figure 6-6). While this doesn't show timing exactly, it at least demonstrates a sense of movement and shows the different states *in context*.

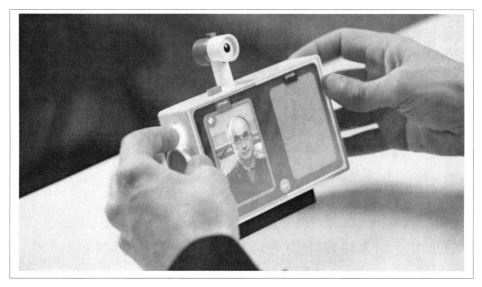

Figure 6-5. A still from a prototype movie. The physical pause button on the left "shoots" a pause indicator out onto the screen. (Courtesy BERG London)

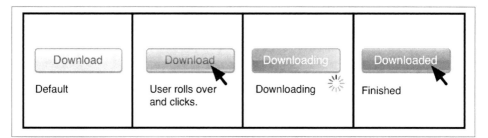

Figure 6-6. An example of a frame-by-frame storyboard

Probably the worst way to document a microinteraction is as static screenshots. Screenshots convey little of the microinteraction's flow, while often removing states from any context that would make them understandable. The best documentation tells a story about what is happening and why.

 To learn more about story-centered design documentation, see "Why good storytelling helps you design great products" (*http://bit.ly/ 12te7iP*), by Braden Kowitz.

If you have to use static screenshots or wireframes, include keyframes into the documentation. Keyframes are a concept that originated with animation, in which the senior animator would draw the essential frames of an animation (the "keyframes"), leaving the parts in between for junior animators to fill in. For microinteractions, keyframes might include the trigger, an essential moment in the rules, and how the microinteraction ends.

It often makes sense to use multiple methods (*http://bit.ly/15odwSq*) to convey a microinteraction: a prototype or movie to show timing, frame-by-frame storyboards for detail and context, and wireframes with keyframes to call out any complicated rules.

Orchestrating Microinteractions

Unless it's a distinct app or device, microinteractions seldom exist alone. More typically, they are found around, inside, or at the center of a larger feature, such as with TaskRabbit's "Post a Task" microinteraction at the beginning of this chapter.

When designing interactions that are not stand-alone, the first action to take is to figure out what the relationship is between the microinteraction and the feature. Does it launch it (logging in), control it (the pause button on a video player), appear inside it (a formatting tool), or end it (the off switch)? Each of these will likely have a very different trigger, and the next thing to determine is how persistent the microinteraction is. That pause button might be there the whole time the app is open, but the formatting tool only appears when the user does something very specific.

What is essential to then determine is if the microinteraction should be a Signature Moment or not; that is, should it be something memorable. In most cases, the answer is no, it should not. It should be pleasing, of course, (which is the point of this book), but rapidity and effortlessness should be the goal, particularly when the microinteraction stands in the way of the overall goal of the product (such as a login microinteraction before the user can actually use the rest of the app).

Turning Microinteractions into Features

Microinteractions can also trigger *other microinteractions*, so that there is a kind of "daisy chain" effect, where one microinteraction can be the trigger for another, which is itself a trigger for another. For example, turning on a device or launching an app (a microinteraction) could be the system trigger to check to see when the user last used the app. If it's been a while, it could launch another microinteraction ("Welcome back, here's what's new since you last used [App]").

This is how you can build features from microinteractions: by orchestrating them so that where one microinteraction leaves off, another picks up. The details are the design.

The trick when working this way, just as with instruments in an orchestra, is to figure out which microinteractions inside the feature get prominence. Not all microinteractions are created equal. Some are important; some should be subtle. Feedback needs to be coordinated to give the right emphasis and to keep the tone consistent.

When designing this way, it can be helpful to have a master list of all the microinteractions that need to be designed to make the feature work properly. This can often be generated from a task list or flow or from functional requirements. From there, you can make a microinteraction map (see Figure 6-7) that shows how the microinteractions all fit together.

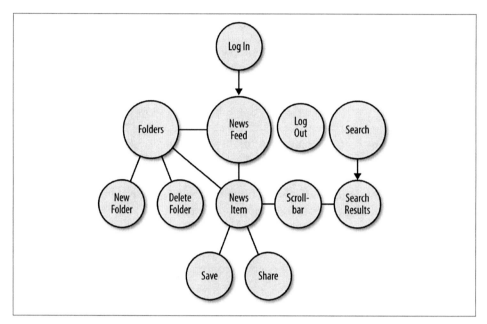

Figure 6-7. A simple example of a microinteractions map for a newsreader.

Pay attention to the handoffs: what microinteraction triggers what microinteraction, and where one microinteraction leaves off and another begins. This might not—in fact, in many cases probably should not—be obvious to the user. You don't want your feature or your overall product to feel like a disjointed collection of tiny moments, but rather like an integrated whole.

It is easy to forget the whole when working this way. After crafting each microinteraction, step back and make sure the piece you just made fits with the other microinteractions. Particularly in sketches or wireframes, it's easy to make a microinteraction that unintentionally conflicts with another microinteraction. For example, working on how a list displays may conflict with how scrolling works. A method to guard against this happening is to note before starting to design a microinteraction which other microinteractions touch it.

Although most of the time we should be concerned that our microinteractions are too much, too intrusive, sometimes they're too dull and need more pizazz.

How to Fix a Dull Microinteraction

We don't always get to start from a clean slate; sometimes there are existing microinteractions in the product we're working on that are just ... there. Or sometimes we've focused on major features and are just now getting around to making our microinteractions shine. But where to begin?

Ask yourself a series of questions based on the principles outlined in this book:

- *Should this be a Signature Moment?* In other words, how memorable should it be? The more memorable, the richer it can be in terms of controls (including custom controls) and feedback.
- *Am I starting from zero?* What do I know about the user or the context that would improve this microinteraction?
- *What is the most important piece of data inside this microinteraction, and can I bring it forward?* What does the user need to know at a glance?
- *Would a custom control be appropriate?* A custom piece of UI practically guarantees the microinteraction will become more prominent.
- *Am I preventing human errors?* If there are any situations where a user can cause an error, what can you do to prevent that automatically?
- *Am I using what is overlooked?* Are there pieces of UI chrome or hardware that could be doing more?
- *Can I make an invisible trigger for advanced users?* Is there a place to make a hidden shortcut (via a gesture or a command key) to get deeper into the rules faster?
- *Are the text and icons human?* Does the microcopy sound like something another human would say out loud? Can you add a touch of humor?
- *Can you add animation to make it less static?* Could you have transitions between screens or states, or an (nonintrusive) indicator of what the next step would be?
- *Can you add additional channels of feedback?* Sound or haptics?
- *Ask what happens when the user returns to the microinteraction the second time. And the hundredth time.* Figure out what the long loop could be.

By answering these questions and applying them to an existing microinteraction, you can't help but make it more engaging. And that's the whole purpose of this book.

Think Small

We've discussed many different microinteractions: the alarm that ruined Mahler's Ninth Symphony, the touchscreen trigger that allows millions to start buying MetroCards for the New York subway, Apple's bungled changes to the rules of Save As, the addictive feedback of slot machines, the loop and mode that almost destroyed a robot on Mars, and how being out of dog food led to a multimillion-dollar business. The small things matter. They always have, and they always will: now perhaps more than ever.

The problems of the 21st century come in all shapes and sizes. Some are massive, systemic problems with no easy solution. Some are small, discrete problems, the solutions to which can offer a brief respite of peace, of humor, or of success. We need people who can work on both kind of problems, big and small, and especially people who can work on both at the same time, making sure the large systems we design—our cities, our governments, our companies, our products—are built for humans. And it's the tiny moments, the microinteractions, that can make these large systems humane. In an era of algorithms and self-driving cars, we need all the humaneness we can get.

Details demonstrate that some care, some thought, some attention has been paid. And this is ultimately what we all want to feel: that some attention has been paid to us and our needs. This is the gift we can give through microinteractions.

Think small, and change the world.

Testing Microinteractions

There are many who would advise you not to bother testing microinteractions, saying they are the equivalent of asking "What color should the bike shed be?" That is: unimportant.[1] Let's assume if you've made it this far into the book, you feel microinteractions have value and can be improved by being validated, tested, and refined via user input.

Microinteractions can benefit from using a Lean UX–style methodology of Build > Measure > Learn: build the microinteraction to test it; measure the design with a variety of quantitative and qualitative methods; learn from an analysis of those findings. Then iterate.[2]

Unlike a true Lean UX process, where you're testing a "Minimum Viable Product" to see if the concepts ("hypotheses") are valuable, with microinteractions we can mostly assume the overall concept is valuable—or at least necessary to the proper functioning of the app or device. You are more testing the *flow and structure* than *testing the concept*. Also dissimilar to Lean UX is the fidelity of the prototype. Rather than prototyping the least you can test (often a paper prototype), with microinteractions, because the structure of microinteractions is important, you need as high a fidelity prototype as you can develop in order to test them effectively. The links between trigger to rules to feedback to loop are tight and not easily separated.

Most microinteractions probably aren't tested alone for desktop software. The effort and expense of setting up and running a testing session (not to mention the effort of building a prototype for testing) are typically too great to test a microinteraction alone for desktop, so they are often lumped together with other items to test. This is not necessarily true for web applications, where prototyping is faster, A/B testing easier to

---

1. "What color should the bike shed be?" is from developer lore. See this link (*http://bit.ly/YA0l9B*) for the whole story.

2. See the book *Lean UX* by Jeff Gothelf (O'Reilly).

try, and analytics more readily available. Mobile applications, too, are getting easier to prototype. If the microinteraction is the whole mobile app, testing is essential; the same is true with devices, although the prototyping for them can be more time-consuming as well.

If statistical relevance is your thing, the bad news is that because microinteractions are small (and thus most changes to them are likewise small), they require more test participants to be relevant. This can mean hundreds (if not thousands) of participants, and it definitely means more than the usual 5–8 participants that many testing sessions have. At the barest minimum, you'll need to aim for at least 20 participants for slightly better data. For the best quantitative data, you need hundreds, thousands, even tens of thousands of users, as is typical for testing on many online sites. If 5% of users open a drop-down, but only 4.75% successfully make a selection, that's very difficult to detect even with thousands of users—and yet it can make a huge difference in sales and adoption.

Unless a microinteraction is terrible or wonderful, determining the statistical effectiveness of its nuances is nigh impossible through qualitative testing. Quantitative is the only real option. For example, adding Google Analytics "Events" to a web microinteraction can give a designer insights into the precise weak points of the microinteraction in a way that could only be done qualitatively by tracking many users over many weeks. That being said, if statistical relevance isn't important to you, even testing with few participants can be illuminating—as always.

As with all product testing, you want to watch out for so-called "scenario errors" that are caused by the test itself. Since testing is an artificial, constructed situation, the setup and guided path the tester takes the user down can cause users to make errors or reveal problems that normal use would not. As just one example, pausing to ask or answer a question can cause crucial feedback to be missed.

What to Look for During Testing

The four most important things to validate with testing are these:

- *That you truly understand the goal of the microinteraction, and not just a step in the process.* The point of setting a status message isn't to type, it's to communicate. Knowing this allows you to fix any emphasis problems, either in the microinteraction itself or in the overall product—how important is this microinteraction to the overall user experience?

- *That you understand what data is important.* This lets you know what data to bring forward and what behavioral-contextual information is valuable to the microinteraction and could be used over time.

- *That any microcopy is necessary, and if so, that it's clear and understood.* This means both instructional copy and, especially, labels.

- *Timing and flow.* Does the microinteraction take too long to perform? Are the loops too long? Too short? Note that long loops that happen over extended periods of time are difficult to test, unless you are doing a longitudinal study, which most developers do not.

The first two are often gleaned from conversation and interviews, the third by observation. But there are many more things to be learned by observation as well, such as:

- *Are there too many clicks/taps/control presses?* In other words, is what the user's trying to do requiring too much effort? This is not necessarily saying count clicks, although that is one measure of effort.
- *Any confusion as to why.* If a user ever says (aloud or via frowning/puzzled looks) "Why am I doing this?" then something is wrong. Usually a label is misnamed, or instructional copy is missing or too vague.
- *What just happened?* This is an indicator of unclear feedback, possibly paired with an unclear label.
- *Did anything just happen?* There is either missing feedback or else the feedback is too subtle.
- *I can't find what I'm looking for.* There is a gap between what the user expects to find and what is there. This is probably a labeling problem, but it could also be that a crucial piece of the microinteraction is missing.
- *I don't know where I am.* This can be a problem with transitions or modes.
- *You just did what to my data/content/input?* This is another case where expectations didn't match the outcome. Either adjust the label or copy, or else this is a deeper, overall problem with the microinteraction in that it might not match what users are trying to accomplish, or else users are uncomfortable with what it does accomplish.
- *If I click/push/tap this, what happens?* This is a case of an unclear label or poor instructional copy.
- *I didn't see that button.* This is a problem with visual hierarchy. The path through the microinteraction isn't visually clear.
- *I didn't know I could do that.* An action is too hidden. This often happens with any multitouch gestures or an invisible trigger such as a key command.
- *What do I do now?* This is the same problem as above: the path isn't clear, especially the next step.
- *What am I seeing there?* This is the result of unclear feedback, usually on a process. Add or clarify with a label, perhaps on a tooltip. This could also mean the data you're showing isn't important.

These are all examples of qualitative data, but quantitative can be useful as well.

Using Quantitative Data

There is an adage (coined by Lord Kelvin) that what can't be measured, can't be improved, and there is some truth to it. Having a baseline—a starting point—and/or something to compare changes to is immeasurably helpful. These are some data points you can test:

Completion rate
> What percent of users were able to complete the microinteraction?

Overall duration of the microinteraction
> How long did it take to complete the microinteraction? (It's often the case that the slowest users can take five to ten times longer to complete tasks than the fastest, so use a geometric mean instead of the median to lessen the effect of this type of extreme value.[3]

Duration of specific steps

Number of steps

Number of clicks/taps/selects
> This is not always instructive but can let you know if something is inefficient.

Number of system errors
> Are there places where the microinteraction fails through no fault of the user? (These are often found when testing on live microinteractions with actual data/connectivity.)

Number of human errors
> These fall into two categories: slips and mistakes. Slips are when the user understands the goal of the action but does something improperly, such as making a typo when entering an email address. A mistake is when a user does not understand the rules and tries something the rules won't allow, such as clicking a header that isn't interactive.[4]

You can also attempt to quantify qualitative data such as by having users rate characteristics like:

---

3. See "8 Core Concepts for Quantifying The User Experience," by Jeff Sauro, *Measuring Usability (http://measuringusability.com)*, December 11, 2012.

4. For more on slips and mistakes, see Norman, Donald, "Design Rules Based on Analyses of Human Error," *Communications of the ACM*, 26, 1983, and *Human Error* by James Reason, 1990.

- Satisfaction
- Difficulty
- Confidence
- Usefulness

on a rated scale (e.g., 1–7, 1 being low, 7 high). However, especially with a small sample size, this can be far from definitive.

This assumes, however, that you will be revising the microinteraction and testing it again to see if there have been improvements, or that you have an alternate version of the same microinteraction to compare with (A/B testing). Again: beware of sample size. A small number of users could make something like an error or a preference seem more (or less) significant than it is.

And even if there is statistical significance, it doesn't mean there is practical significance. The most important lesson about using data to help design is this: it can't design for you. Data requires a human being to interpret it, and then place it into context. Data will seldom tell you *why* something is happening.

The data needs to be made meaningful, which sometimes means ignoring it. Why would you ever ignore data? Here's the simplest example: most online advertising isn't clicked. If you get a 0.5% clickthrough rate, you're often doing very well.[5] So should we remove all online ads, since they are so seldom used? 99.9% of users think so (the other 0.1% of people work for advertising agencies). But getting rid of advertising would essentially mean getting rid of the site itself, as there would be no money to operate it. Would you like Google to go away? You can't listen to the data entirely because the data doesn't understand the overall context: the business and organizational environment and the user base that are more than just numbers on a spreadsheet. Data should be an input to your decision making, not the decider alone.

A Process for Testing Microinteractions

The following is one possible process for testing microinteractions that could be followed. It is certainly not the only process, but it could be a starting point:

1. Before showing participants any prototypes, ask them how they expect the microinteraction to work. Ask if they've ever used anything similar in the past. Ask what the one thing is that they want to accomplish by using this microinteraction. Check if there is anything they would want to know before using the microinteraction—

---

5. See, for example, "So Many Ads, So Few Clicks," *BusinessWeek*, November 11, 2007.

if there is one piece of information that would make using the microinteraction unnecessary.

2. Have them use the microinteraction unaided. Any quantitative data should be collected at this point, and/or immediately after.

3. Go through the microinteraction with the user step by step, having the participant talk out loud about any impressions and decisions. See if participants can explain how the microinteraction works (the rules). Note any discrepancies.

4. Ask if they came back tomorrow, what would they want the microinteraction to remember about them.

5. End by asking what one thing should be fixed.

With this process, you should be able to uncover and diagnose any issues with the microinteraction, as well as validate any of the overall goals and needs. I recommend doing this process at least twice, with two sets of participants, revising the microinteraction based on user feedback and findings analysis between sets.

Index

We'd like to hear your suggestions for improving our indexes. Send email to index@oreilly.com.

errors
    feedback regarding, 88, 94, 101
    initiating system triggers, 44
    preventing, 74
    quantitative data regarding, 144

F

features
    compared to microinteractions, 4–5
    microinteractions becoming, 137–139
    relationship to microinteractions, 137
feedback, 14, 17–18
    alarm app example of, 128
    amount of, 86–88, 92
    dishwasher control panel example of, 133,
       134
    for errors, 88, 94, 101
    method of delivery, 90–92
        audio, 101–104
        haptics, 104–105
        visual, 96–101
    personality conveyed by, 18, 93–96
    relevance to situation, 92
    rules communicated by, 54, 86–86
    rules for, 54, 106–107
    shared playlist example of, 130
    Siri example of, 94
    situations requiring, 88–90
    slot machine example of, 85–86
finger motions (see gestures)
fonts used in this book, xi
For loops, 114
form fields, 29

G

geons, 31
gestures, 28
    as invisible triggers, 33
    tap state, of manual trigger, 37
Goldberg, Adele (developer)
    scrollbars, 10
Gypsy application example, 9

H

haptic feedback, 104–105
hover state, of manual trigger, 37

I

in process state, of manual trigger, 37
incoming data, initiating system triggers, 44
infinite loops, 115
Ingalls, Dan (developer)
    scrollbars, 10
internal data, initiating system triggers, 44
invisible manual triggers, 32–36, 74
invitation state, of screen object, 62
iPhone mobile app example, 126–129

K

Kay, Alan (developer)
    scrollbars, 10
keyboard shortcuts, as redundant triggers, 74
Koomey's Law, 12
Kryder's Law, 12

L

labels, 39–42, 77
Law of the Conservation of Complexity, 67
Lean UX process, for testing, 141
location, geographic, initiating system triggers,
    44
long loops, 117–120
The Long Wow, 118
loops, 14, 18, 114–120
    alarm app example of, 128
    dishwasher control panel example of, 134
    length of, 115
    long loops, 117–120
    Mars Spirit rover example of, 110
    rules for, 54
    shared playlist example of, 131
    types of, 114

M

manual triggers, 26–42
    components of, 28–42
    consistent action taken by, 26
    controls for, 28–36
    corresponding to system triggers, 45
    discoverability of, 29–31
    information shown by, 27–28
    invisible, 32–36, 74
    labels for, 39–42, 77
    states of, 37–38

About the Author

Dan Saffer is a director of interaction design at Smart Design. He is the author of *Designing for Interaction: Creating Innovative Applications and Devices* (New Riders), *Designing Gestural Interfaces* (O'Reilly), and the Amazon ebook Designing Devices (*http://amzn.to/11nqV7K*). Since 1995, he has designed appliances, devices, software, websites, robots, and services that are used by millions of people every day.

Colophon

There are two species of sparrow on the cover of *Microinteractions*: the English sparrow (*Passer domesticus*) and the American tree sparrow (*Spizella arborea*). Although these two sparrows look alike, they come from different genera.

The English sparrow, or House sparrow, is more closely related to the Eurasian tree sparrow (*Passer montanus*) than it is to the American tree sparrow. The English sparrow has a round head, a plump body, short legs, and averages 16 cm in length. While it is native to Europe, Asia, and North Africa, it has the widest geographical spread of any non-domestic bird, in large part due to its introduction to North America in 1851.

Far from being an endangered species, the English sparrow is considered a pest in many places. It is commonly found in settled areas and will flock to bird feeders, displacing rarer birds that the feeders are intended to attract. English sparrows mate in monogamous pairs, although not every sparrow chooses a mate upon maturity. Instead, some sparrows serve as helpers for a breeding pair, increasing the likelihood of there being a replacement mate if one of the pair dies. English sparrows make their nests in and around human dwellings, and will sometimes evict other birds in order to occupy their nests.

The American tree sparrow resembles the English sparrow, but is more closely related to other American sparrows, such as the Chipping sparrow and Brewer's sparrow. It is about the same size as the English sparrow and has a rust-colored cap and eyeline, as opposed to the Eurasian tree sparrow, which has a black throat and eyeline. The American tree sparrow's layers of fat protect it from its frigid tundra environment, where it spends the summer months in northern Canada and Alaska. In the winter, it migrates to southern Canada and the northern United States.

Ironically, the American tree sparrow does not generally inhabit trees, which are uncommon on the tundra, preferring shrubs and even open grassland during migrations. The American tree sparrow will shake seeds loose from a plant by flapping its wings, as well as pecking at the ground to find insects and berries. It is a social bird, congregating in small flocks, but makes less noise than the vociferous English sparrow.

The cover image is from Wood's *Animate Creation*. The cover font is Adobe ITC Garamond. The text font is Adobe Minion Pro; the heading font is Adobe Myriad Condensed; and the code font is Dalton Maag's Ubuntu Mono.

Get even more for your money.

Join the O'Reilly Community, and register the O'Reilly books you own. It's free, and you'll get:

- $4.99 ebook upgrade offer
- 40% upgrade offer on O'Reilly print books
- Membership discounts on books and events
- Free lifetime updates to ebooks and videos
- Multiple ebook formats, DRM FREE
- Participation in the O'Reilly community
- Newsletters
- Account management
- 100% Satisfaction Guarantee

Signing up is easy:

1. **Go to: oreilly.com/go/register**
2. **Create an O'Reilly login.**
3. **Provide your address.**
4. **Register your books.**

Note: English-language books only

To order books online:
oreilly.com/store

For questions about products or an order:
orders@oreilly.com

To sign up to get topic-specific email announcements and/or news about upcoming books, conferences, special offers, and new technologies:
elists@oreilly.com

For technical questions about book content:
booktech@oreilly.com

To submit new book proposals to our editors:
proposals@oreilly.com

O'Reilly books are available in multiple DRM-free ebook formats. For more information:
oreilly.com/ebooks

Spreading the knowledge of innovators   oreilly.com

CPSIA information can be obtained at www.ICGtesting.com
Printed in the USA
BVOW062024160513

320930BV00002B/2/P